Red Sox Fans
Are from Mars,
Yankees Fans
Are from Uranus

Why Red Sox Fans Are Smarter,
Funnier, and Better Looking
(In Language Even Yankees
Fans Can Understand)

Andy Wasif

TRIUMPH
B O O K S

Library of Congress Cataloging-in-Publication Data

Wasif, Andy.
Red Sox fans are from Mars, Yankees fans are from Uranus / Andy Wasif.
p. cm.
ISBN 978-1-60078-347-0
1. Boston Red Sox (Baseball team)—Humor 2. Baseball fans—Massachusetts—Boston—Humor. 3. New York Yankees (Baseball team)—Humor. 4. Baseball fans—New York (State)—New York—Humor. 5. Sports rivalries—United States. I. Title.
GV875.B62W349 2010
796.357'640974—dc22
                    2009050717

This book is available in quantity at special discounts for your group or organization. For further information, contact:
Triumph Books
542 South Dearborn Street
Suite 750
Chicago, Illinois 60605
(312) 939–3330
Fax (312) 663–3557
www.triumphbooks.com

Printed in U.S.A.
ISBN: 978-1-60078-347-0
Design by Sue Knopf
Page production by Patricia Frey
Photos courtesy of AP Images unless otherwise indicated
Illustrations by Vito Sabsay

Contents

Introduction

The year was 2003. For many, it represented a low point in their lives. (Or the *last* point in their lives, if the stunning turn of events about to transpire literally killed them.) For many others, it was just par for the course, another sad sticker in the sports passports of their lives.

Fans of the Boston Red Sox and New York Yankees lined the streets of their respective cities, peering into bars and trying to get a glimpse of any television set playing each game of the American League Championship Series.

Pedro Martinez threw at Jorge Posada as he pointed at his head, Roger Clemens threw over Manny Ramirez's head, Don Zimmer attacked Martinez and was tossed on his head, and the head of security ate a head of lettuce as part of his leafy green diet.

Before it was all over, onlookers watched as benches emptied, Tanyon Sturtze attacked Gabe Kapler from behind, David Ortiz tossed Sturtze, and Grady Little left Pedro in one inning too long.

And with that, Red Sox fans had come the closest they had been since 1904 to defeating the Yankees in a game that mattered. But now there was much more at stake—85 years of futility and decades of torment, to be precise. Emotions had bubbled close to dangerous levels.

I felt so powerless to do anything. The Red Sox had lost. Had I lost anything? I checked my bank account. Still empty. I went through the

CD cases in my car. The CDs were still there, even after the valets had parked my car. So technically, no, I hadn't lost anything. Yet, I was the one who would be made the fool at the hands of Yankees fans...and these were my *friends*. It just wasn't fair.

Then, just when it seemed things couldn't get any more heated, the war between the two factions escalated. Curt Schilling, who had been bound for New York, ended up in Boston; Alex Rodriguez, all but sealed in a package to Boston, got rerouted to New York; Ben Affleck ran to the airwaves to rant about it; New Kids on the Block had not yet reunited; and George Steinbrenner, the tuti capo of the Yankees organization, continued to fire verbal salvos at the Red Sox and their CEO, Larry Lucchino. Fans could only sit and wait.

For the next seven months, small battles broke out. Jason Varitek shoved his mitt into A-Rod's face, Nomar left town, Papi smashed a few walk-offs, Bill Mueller hit some doubles, a first baseman sang karaoke in his underwear, a gaggle of Idiots incited lunacy throughout a town, and the Yankees held off the Red Sox down the stretch—again—to win the American League East crown.

Fast-forward to September of 2004. The Yankees and Red Sox were in the middle of yet another tight pennant race. Though MLB commissioner Bud Selig's insane unbalanced schedule had caused the two teams to face each other approximately 122 times during the 162-game season, this series between the two bloodthirsty rivals had a particularly rancorous feeling to it.

KEY TERMS

Larry Lucchino—current CEO of the Red Sox and frequent instigator of verbal battles with the Steinbrenners

I found myself in Philadelphia for a wedding weekend. Next to me was my best friend, a Yankees fan. We'll call him Chuck. (Even though his name is Jerry.) Chuck and I had been friends since the early 1990s. At the time, the Red Sox could not beat Dave Stewart or any of the other A's pitchers, and the Yankees were rambling on incoherently about Don Mattingly, a guy who had never been on a winning playoff team. Players hadn't yet discovered "the juice" and, in 1994, owners decided to ruin Tony Gwynn's best shot at batting .400 and Ken Griffey Jr.'s chance to become the only legitimate slugger to hit more than 61 home runs in a season. Baseball had a work stoppage—the dreaded strike. So after a decade of bell-bottoms and epic pennant-race collapses, the animosity between Boston and New York was dormant for a while. And with our guards down, Chuck and I became friends. It's as the ancient Sumerians used to say: "Let your guard down for a second, and the rest of your life will be miserable."

Eventually, the owners recanted and allowed the players back onto their fields, but the players had to be willing to accept more money and eliminate any thought of a salary cap. The players begrudgingly agreed and then raucously celebrated their rotten luck.

It turned out to be a blessing in disguise for all the major league teams that were based in a northern borough of New York City and liked to throw money around like they were at the county fair's "Money Toss" event. The Yankees spent and won and spent and won. Red Sox fans were powerless to do anything thanks to the Yawkey Trust (which was in place to trust that no championship would be won under its ownership) and Yankees fans were emboldened again with the days of Steve Balboni and Steve Howe (after his seventh *lifetime* suspension) just a distant memory.

These Bronxians took every opportunity to remind Fenwayites of their futility in trying to compete for a championship by chanting "1918!" It happened at ballgames, at backyard barbecues, on subway rides, in prison cafeterias, at Catholic baptisms…anywhere and everywhere a fan of the Red Sox appeared near a fan of the Yankees.

So the evening before the wedding in Philadelphia, Chuck and I were at the hotel lounge, having a grand old time slipping different condiments and various spices into each other's beverages without the other noticing, when the score from that night's Red Sox/Yankees contest appeared on the TV above the bar.

The Red Sox were in second place, trailing by 4.5 games but close enough to take the division with a final surge. The only thing lying in their way were the Yankees who, the score informed us, had won that evening by a score of 6–4.

Well, with so much at stake, my friend turned to me and started yelling right in my ear, "THEEEEEEEE YANKEEZ WIN! THEEEEEEEE YANKEEZ WIN!"

Parents walking by grabbed their children and herded them toward safer territory. The bartenders took cover behind the bar as though we were in a Wild West saloon. Smoke alarms began going off.

Yet, I stood there staring straight ahead, waiting for him to take a breath. Then I calmly said, "It's only the regular season. The playoffs are what matter."

He replied, in his best Yankees-style mocking tone, "Yeah, the playoffs! We'll see about the playoffs! Just like last year, baby! Woo!" And then I think his head exploded, I can't quite recall.

The next night, the night of the wedding, Chuck and I were seated together at the same table, ironically Table 5, which he pointed out was the total number of championships the Red Sox had won, compared to the Yankees' 26. I was so glad he was there to point that out.

The score of the second game of the series came over on someone's BlackBerry: the Red Sox had won 12–5. Now, you'd think that I would get to chant something like "THEEEEEEEE RED SOX WIN!" but I decided to keep my emotions in check. I did not want to have to pay for any celebrating later. (As the ancient Phoenicians used to say, "Payback is a female dog.")

But I didn't even get the chance to enjoy the moment, for Chuck was again screaming in my ear, this time saying, "IT DOESN'T MATTER, IT'S ONLY THE REGULAR SEASON!" regurgitating the phrase I had used the night before. I thought a loss would quiet my friend, but alas, he is a Yankees fan.

Throughout the Electric Slide and Hora dances, I stewed at Chuck, at my standing as a Red Sox fan, and at the weird cousin of the bride sitting next to me who didn't know his left from his right. But then a light went on inside of me; I had an epiphany. (Luckily, I took a swig of Pepto-Bismol and it went away.)

For the first time in my life, I truly understood Yankees fans—26 championships in the previous 80 years to my club's zero, yet they still needed to belittle and abuse me. New York fans wanted to keep their feet on the proverbial throat of Red Sox Nation, and by proverbial, I mean *actual* in most cases. But they had a sense that it was all slipping away. The Red Sox were finally a real threat to them.

I didn't realize it at the time, but I was witnessing something I'd not seen before, an emotion Yankees fans had no experience emitting—fear. The Yankees were afraid of losing their stronghold, of losing their ability to mock and devalue Red Sox fans, and most of all, of losing their favorite chant, the one that begins with "19" and ends with "18."

My feelings toward Chuck had suddenly turned from anger and resentment to sorrow and sympathy. After taking a champagne bottle out of an ice bucket and dumping the ice on him, I actually felt a twinge of remorse. So, as he toweled off, I went back to get the bottle. I brought it over to him and poured him a glass and apologized. Then I dumped the remainder of the bottle on his head. It's like the modern Bostonians always say: "Never share champagne with a Yankees fan, unless they are soaking in it."

After that wedding (where the cake was absolutely fantastic, by the way—I only wish we had eaten it instead of starting the banquet hall's first food fight), I wondered how I had not seen his fan frailties before. In the heat of a typical baseball season, you get caught up in emotions. As a Red Sox fan, I was always predisposed to take up a defensive position, ready to lash out at the taunts.

During the previous 12 years, our friendship had been different. The most heated we had ever become was over why our teams insisted on dumping, then reacquiring, catchers Rick Cerone and Mike Stanley at different times. It was at that moment that I realized that neither of us was wrong...but neither of us was right either. We'd been going in a never-ending cycle. I just didn't understand him and his actions. I wanted to learn more.

(Of course, I did actually end up being right. The regular season did *not* matter and the playoffs did, just as I had suggested. I'm just saying.)

Though the tide had finally turned, thus alleviating a lot of the sting from years and years and years (and years) of traumatic teasing that I could not control, it did nothing to cease the never-ending back-and-forth bickering between Yankees and Red Sox fans.

The following questions maintain the foundation for a lifetime of unanswerable brain stumpers:

- Which team has suffered the greatest choke job?
- Was Joe Torre a better manager than Tito Francona?

- Are the Yankees hurting baseball?
- Have the Red Sox become the new Yankees?
- Which team has more fair-weather fans?
- Was Joe DiMaggio better than Ted Williams?
- Which fans are more obnoxious?
- Whose stadium is nicer?
- Does George Steinbrenner really smell like sulfur?
- Do the tears of Red Sox fans cause earthquakes?

And the list goes on.

As Chuck finally toweled off and rejoined us at the bar, I decided to spend time researching the subjects. (Well, it was actually shortly after I changed my clothes following Chuck's sneak attack with the drink gun he grabbed from behind the bar.) And so, over the past five years, I have dedicated my life to such pursuits.

I became an "interfanatical relationship counselor," and my practice has blossomed thanks to an influx of Red Sox and Yankees fans who could not bear to spend time around the other. They have given me a firsthand look at the cases you see and experience every day, citing their irreconcilable differences and the fact that they are too set in their ways to change their relationships now. There is no way they can continue any sort of discourse.

"Her team deserves to be stripped of their championships, while mine does not."

"He keeps yelling '1918!'"

"He says we're a bunch of pathetic, bellyaching babies."

"She's whining about our irresponsible spending!"

"I can name more players on my team than she can on hers!"

"She takes the name of Ted Williams in vain, in front of our children, no less!"

And it's not just married couples. It's relatives, friends, public officials, mail recipients on a mail carrier's route, and coworkers. Did you know that Yahoo! and Microsoft would never have merged their search engine functions if not for some counseling sessions in my office?

I've learned much from studying the fans, researching what makes them tick, why they say what they say—believe me, I've heard it all. And like I did at one time, each fan believes he or she is right and the other fan is wrong. My job is not to get them to adopt the other's team, but to get them to see where the other is coming from. One of my favorite methods is to practice role-playing.

In order to better formulate these theories, I decided to walk a mile in the shoes of Yankees fans—their sweaty, hole-laden, and worn-down shoes. I went to New York City, bought a Derek Jeter jersey, and wore it everywhere. (I did have a "Big Papi" shirt on underneath, sort of like wearing a garlic necklace when hanging at Dracula's house.)

I spent time talking about how much better Curtis Granderson is than Johnny Damon. I walked around humming "New York, New York." I set my Boston friend's hat on fire. I talked about Yogi and the Mick like they were friends of mine. I quoted Billy Crystal movies more than Ben Affleck flicks. I bowed toward the east every time Joe Torre's name was mentioned. I pushed my cousin from Boston out of my car while heading over the Verrazano Bridge. I talked about what a festering, rat-infested sewage pit Boston was. I even willingly shelled out $10.75 for a mediocre cheesesteak at Yankee Stadium.

For a while, I *was* a Yankees fan.

When my experiment was over, I took a kerosene bath and sat back to review what I had learned. I realized that Red Sox and Yankees fans are so different, they are almost the same. It's like traveling tens of thousands of miles east, only to find you've arrived just a few miles west of where you started. This realization has allowed me to use what I'd learned to help others in need.

Two brothers-in-law, Bruno and Sully, once came to me with their problems. Their wives, two sisters, were not familiar with the conflagration raging throughout their region, more content to watch *American Idol* than America's pastime. But Bruno's wife Gina had her blissful ignorance shattered—along with their TV—after Mariano Rivera blew a five-out save, an event that prompted Bruno to throw his beer bottle at their plasma screen.

Sully tormented Bruno by newspapering his car with clippings from the *Daily News* reliving the night's collapse (note: this was back when people actually bought newspapers). Bruno, in turn, backed his car through Sully's fence, claiming he couldn't see out his rearview mirror because the panels of *Marmaduke* were in his way.

Each felt that there was no way to get through to the other. To them, their situation seemed hopeless. But in just one session with me, they began to see each other in a new light. One of the methods I employed in our session was role-playing: I had Bruno newspaper Sully's car and then had Sully drive into Bruno's fence.

"How did that make you feel?" I asked Bruno, knowing the response.

"Pretty much the same. I still hate him, but now I *understand* him," he said. Sully and Bruno realized they were both lashing out in the same manner, and had the situation been different—if Jonathan Papelbon had blown the save instead of Rivera, for example—Bruno would have been the instiga*tor* instead of the instiga*tee*.

Disputes like this are not random by any stretch of the imagination. They happen again and again. The names are different (well, except in the case of Sully or Fitzy in Boston and Tony or Sal in the Bronx), but everyone is acting exactly as you would expect them to act. So, how can you end all the car-papering and fence-smashing in your own life?

This book will provide you with the preventative techniques you'll need to avoid such situations, as well as the insight you'll need to understand your antagonists. I will not delve into anthropology, biology, pathology, cosmology, or any other -ologies to explain why we are different, partially because I don't know what those mean and partially because this is not that type of book. The title *Red Sox Fans Are from Mars, Yankees Fans Are from Uranus* refers to fans being from different places, having different experiences, and acting because of different motivations; it is not an accurate description of birthplace. I do not believe Yankees fans are *actually* from Uranus. Uranus cannot support any form of life, to start with. Mars, however, has been found to contain evidence of water, a necessary ingredient in beer. Therefore, it is not outside the realm of possibility that Red Sox fans are, indeed, from Mars…albeit a very slight one.

Let's face it—Red Sox and Yankees fans are stuck in this relationship, so you might as well make the most of it. The baseball season is a long one—it typically lasts 842 days a year, and that's not counting rainouts. During that time, there are twists and turns, hopes raised and dashed, walk-offs hit and saves blown, which cause the rules of engagement to constantly change. At one moment, Boston fans are on top of the world, able to berate the Yankees fans morning, noon, and game time, for their team rules the other. But then, a lightning storm knocks out power for a couple of hours and when it returns, they find the Red Sox four games back and their phones are besieged by calls from New Yorkers unleashing their full arsenal of offensive rhetoric.

I often use generalities to illuminate the entire picture. You are more inclined to believe that I'm dead-on when commenting about your opponent than you are when I make a judgment about you. That's to be expected. And not everyone falls neatly into each type or shares the same beliefs; that's why some Yankees fans also root for the Patriots. Although the benefits of this book can help on many levels, the deepest and most passionate fans should still seek counseling and some type of anger-management seminar from a licensed professional, probably not a baseball fan. Or you can only speak to one another between November and February. That is up to you. In fact, if you can avoid one another during the spring and summer months, it might make your life easier. Though I would certainly still read this book cover to cover. What have you got to lose? You've made it this far, right?

It is my pleasure to share the things I have learned with you. And with this enlightening tutorial, may the steroids of success and kindness be injected into the buttocks of your life.

1

Red Sox Fans Are from Mars, Yankees Fans Are from Uranus

Bostonians and New Yorkers. They are not that different, on the outside. But on the inside? Yecch! You do *not* want to get a look in there.

You might be asking yourself, "Am I really from Mars? Let me check my birth certificate." Or you might be saying, "I don't remember my grandfather telling me he was from Uranus." You know what? Just go with it. I'll explain it to you later.

In order to picture early Red Sox fans living on Mars and the early Yankees fans on Uranus, we must first know a thing or two about the histories of each group.

Boston/Mars

Boston was known as the "City by the Bay" before San Francisco came along and stole the name. (I mean, we *are* the "Bay State," fer cryin' out loud. And it ain't because of Stockbridge.) Boston was the center for politics, commerce, education, and those trashy romance novels set against pre-Elizabethan backdrops; if anything happened, it happened in Boston, and, if you knew what was good for you, it *stayed* in Boston. Originally a narrow peninsula known as the Shawmut Peninsula, Baybank bought it and renamed it. They were bought out by Fleet Bank, and after one more sale the name became the Banknorth Peninsula, which loosely translates in Wallomollopoag Indian to "Boston."

It wasn't until the mid-19th century that Bostonians decided they needed more room to live and proceeded to cover over the marshy bogs (no relation to former Red Sox third baseman and Hall of Famer Wade Boggs) with landfill, thereby tripling the city's size and causing those nerds from Cambridge to walk farther after dinner and cannoli at the North End.

After democracy took hold, there wasn't much left to gripe about in the taverns and halls. Boston was at a crossroads. The denizens tried to develop a passion for the bean-eating contests of the mid-1840s and for the horse parade celebrating the centennial of 1876, but nothing quite caught their interest until the advent of subways allowed Boston University fraternity students to pack themselves into train cars like sardines.

Alas, even that left something to be desired.

New York/Uranus

New York City is actually made up of five islands (three of which weren't actually islands at all, but just said they were so they could claim the "island status" exemption on their taxes). One island, Staten Island, was first visited by Giovanni da Verrazano, an Italian employed by the king of France, who after becoming the first free-agent explorer opted to take more money to work for another country. Fitting that he would end up in New York.

Manhattan, on the other hand, was founded by the Dutch (after the Manhattes Indians lived there) almost a century later. Adriaen Block lived there because his ship had been destroyed by fire (no doubt set by early Yankees fans). One year later, he built a new ship and left, complaining, "This place smells like feet." It soon turned into a quaint community where overworked English citizens could go on vacation.

Ask the Doctor

Q: I read your previous book *Mars/Uranus: Dealing with Playoff Defeat* and bought a stress-relieving ball for my office as you recommended. My coworker and cube neighbor was relentless from the moment the Yankees signed three big free agents, however, and by the time September rolled around, my forearms were as big as tree trunks and my stress ball was flat. What should I do now?

A: I would consider entering one of those strength competitions, assuming you can also pull a tractor with your hair. Short of that, try squeezing something that won't lose its elasticity, like a pillow. A pillow is also great for muffling your screams and won't kill your coworker if you use it as a projectile.

In a move that would have made George Steinbrenner proud, the Dutch purchased Manhattan (which comes from the Manhattan Algonquin term meaning, "I'm walkin' here!") for nothing more than the modern equivalent of $24, or the price of a hamburger in Midtown. Meanwhile, Jonas Bronck was tending his small, 500-acre farm, not suspecting it would one day become the home of the most celebrated team in sports and a meeting place for tens of thousands of fans, taking the same personal freedoms in the street as the farm animals did three centuries earlier.

What began as home to a mere 1,300 people has become a metropolis with an estimated population of 300 billion, most of whom ride the same subway as I do. New York has become the epicenter of the country, if not the world. But for many years, before organized sports had captured the public's imagination, New York had no real identity and its citizens were jealous. The city's politics and commerce were not as dynamic as Boston's or Philadelphia's, the latter also having a grasp on the historic landmark market. However, the first White House was in New York. It just didn't stay there when George Washington realized the price of everything was insane.

A New Hobby

So how did our respective cities turn us into who we are today? Well, to understand that, we must first remember that Boston was at one point the hub of America, hence its nickname—Beantown. New York still needed to find itself; at the time, no one really cared to live on an island in the middle of nowhere. That would all change with a little rawhide, some wood, and a few stuffed canvas sacks.

By the end of the 1800s, a new pastime was taking hold—cow tipping. The fields of the Northeast were lush and the cows were vulnerable, so it was a perfect match. But since no leagues were set up, cow tipping was hard to gamble on, so locals kept their eyes open for any other activities. They soon found and became enamored with a game that had its roots in the English games of rounders and cricket. Early American versions of this sport took a little from column A and a little

KEY TERMS

Abner Doubleday—former Union Army general who for generations was generally recognized as the undisputed inventor of the modern game of baseball

Alexander Cartwright—a bookseller and volunteer firefighter who is the **actual** inventor of the modern game of baseball

from column B and played it in New England, where it was called "the Massachusetts game."

It was Alexander Cartwright who grabbed onto the new hybrid. Then Abner Doubleday switched the name on the patent application to include his instead of Cartwright's, thus inserting himself into the history books as the man who invented it. He deemed to call it baseball because it utilized bases and balls. (Other names considered, but ultimately rejected, include "batstrike," "cleatcup," and "moundplate.") Humorist Robert Benchley, commenting on the discrepancies between the two sports, put his support behind the new game when he said, "England and America should scrap cricket and baseball, and come up with a new game that they can both play. Like baseball, for example."

And so the British game of rounders had popped the pond—along with tons of Irish looking for a decent steak fry—and taken up shop here in America. Leagues were formed, including the very popular National League, or "senior circuit" as it's come to be known because everyone playing in it eats dinner at 4:00 PM.

Boston (the Beaneaters, who were formerly the Red Caps, and would go on to become the Rustlers, the Doves, the Bees, and finally the Braves) and New York (the Giants, formerly the Gothams) had teams, but for some reason, there was no warring tone. No one sitting in the stands really cared enough to get worked into a frenzy over any silly songs sung in a mocking tone toward the other team during games.

Then, a new upstart league was founded, and again Boston became the gold standard. The team got off to a fantastic start, winning the first World Series and five of the first 15. New York again was covetous and strove to outdo its elder brother.

A Change in the Air

Cities for the new American League teams were determined by the commissioner of the league, Ban Johnson. He selected, among them, Boston and Baltimore. Soon, Baltimore's mayor lost a bet with New York's mayor over how many corrupt politicians he could place into office (New York's mayor far exceeded the Baltimore mayor's estimation) and the Orioles were sent to New York, where they became the Highlanders because the team had "the quickening."

For a while, Boston remained in charge, the tops at everything. The two rivals seemed relatively content to coexist…at first. Then New York closed the gap. The younger brother was very competitive and within two decades had turned the tables with a lot of player acquisitions from Boston and a little bit of moxie (which was considered a performance-enhancing drug back in the day, but wasn't banned by the league since it was available over the counter).

The new pastime had a new king. New York, now named the Yankees, had begun to win and win often (if you call a minuscule 25 percent of the time "often"). As a result of that astounding success rate, their fans became arrogant and developed a disturbing feeling of entitlement. Couple that with the abrasive attitude inherent in New Yorkers and you've got the seeds for a cauldron of dislike.

Boston, on the other hand, became wanton. After a brief surge to begin the century, they hit a dry spell. Unable to win a championship changed Bostonians from proud leaders to paranoid wannabes, and because the Yankees' run of dominance was kickstarted by players from Boston, the City by the Bay harbored much ill will for New York. Fans slinked back to the more than 7,000 Ivy League schools located within their borders and immersed themselves in their opinions. Most of those opinions, however, still had to do with the Yankees.

Planetary Rivals

Mars is known as the "red planet," or in this case the "Red Sox planet." Named for the ancient Roman god of war (whose name was actually Harold, but his brother had trouble pronouncing that so called him "Mars" instead), it takes less than two years to travel around the sun and each day is exactly 24 hours and 39 minutes long, or roughly the duration of a typical Yankees–Red Sox game.

Uranus, or "the pinstriped planet" as it's called in some circles, was named for the first god of the sky. The ancient Greek poet Hesiod said that Uranus had no father. Hence, when Pedro said "Guess the Yankees are my daddy," it struck close to home as Yankees fans were excited to be the father they never had. It takes Uranus more than 84 years to orbit the sun, or what used to be the length of time between Red Sox championships. The average temperature on the surface is 4,200 degrees Fahrenheit. (The fact that Mars is an average -80 degrees Fahrenheit helps explain why the clash between the two teams in 2004 led to so many "Hell Freezes Over" headlines.) Also, Uranus is composed of 83 percent hydrogen, 15 percent helium, and 2 percent methane, which would explain the smell on the Upper East Side.

For the purposes of this book, I am using the term *Martians* to describe fanatics of the Boston Red Sox and *Uranians* (Urasites? The Uranese? Uranusians? Let's just go with Uranians) to depict those rooting for the New York Yankees. It took a few years for Martians to build up animosity for their rivals. Similarly, it took a few years for Uranians to realize they had become dominant over their counterparts. It is that history, coupled with the way of life in both cities, that shaped the personalities and demeanors inherent in both fan bases. Their cognitive development, though coming from the same birth mother, so to speak, was almost totally opposite.

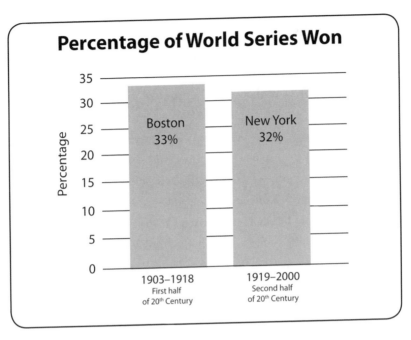

As you can see in this chart, the pendulum of success swung entirely from one side to the other in the middle of the 20th century. Boston won early and then gave way to the cold-hearted efficiency of the Yankees through most of the remaining decades.

The Hormones Made Me Do It

Environment and experience play a role in the evolution (or lack thereof) of both fan bases, and our hormonal development is different as well. For each fan, puberty comes early in adolescence, usually around the third or fourth game he or she attends. Being in the largest city in the country, New Yorkers had to adapt quickly to their "show no mercy" environment. Thus, they react more aggressively to outside threats, whether it be jockeying for a seat on the subway or sucker punching a Red Sox fan who alludes to the Yankees' lack of championships between 2000 and 2009.

Impulses shoot down through the thoracic cavity, which secretes a chemical called "brutoxin" that makes Yankees fans shout and puff out their chests at a moment's notice. For some, the extra burst of brutoxin allows them to dislodge their jaws more than twice as wide as other fans, enabling them to cheer and shout louder than those around them.

Red Sox fans' brutoxin levels are very low, but it is available in an over-the-counter supplement in the event they plan to come in contact with a Yankees fan. (Be sure to follow the dosage instructions; otherwise, you might actually *become* a Yankees fan.) Boston fans did develop a hormone that made them put the letter *r* on the end of words ending in *a* and the letter *a* on the end of words ending in *r*. It's called "arrarraran." This hormone causes Martians to say things like "Franconer

KEY TERMS

Brutoxin—a hormone found in Uranians that makes them behave brutishly

Arrarraran—a hormone found in Martians that forces misuse of the letters **a** and **r**

has a big dilemmer as to whethah aw nawt to pitch Jonny Lestah in Game Foah which could be the clinchah," speech that often confounds Yankees fans and further exacerbates the frosty relations.

Fans from both cities also produce a chemical called "lootesin," which causes them to break glass and light fires during moments of celebration. It also makes it easier for them to climb up lamp posts.

These various hormones affected the brains of both Martians and Uranians differently over time, as we can see from the scientific diagrams on page 11.

Both brains contain a primary fear cortex, though in a Martian brain, it's a much larger area than in a Uranian brain. Martians have also developed a unique area known as Massarotti's Area (in the left hemisphere). It's where the panic button is stored and activated when needed.

These small differences may not seem that significant, but even the smallest discrepancy creates an entirely unique set of behaviors and perspectives. That is why if you ask fans if they are similar to their counterpart, the answers are mixed. Red Sox fans would answer with

KEY TERMS

Lootesin—a chemical found in Martians and Uranians that causes them to break glass and light fires during moments of celebration. It also makes it easier for them to climb up lamp posts

Massarotti's Area—the part of a Martian's brain responsible for panic and paranoia. It provides the ability to turn any molehill into a mountain with hypothetical doomsday scenarios

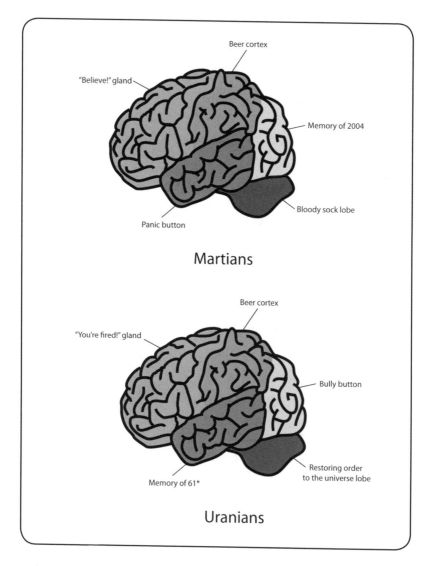

a sharp "No!" while Yankees fans would answer "No!" and give you an atomic wedgie. However, if told that Red Sox fans had already answered in the negative, Yankees fans might change their response by adding, "They haven't won 27 championships."

How the World Views Us

One of the great disagreements between Martians and Uranians is, who are the better fans? It is impossible to answer objectively without input from other baseball fans. Thus, using their opinions as part of an intricate, weighted rating system that includes factors such as player knowledge, game etiquette, ritual adherence, eating habits, and the like, the following definitive answer was reached:

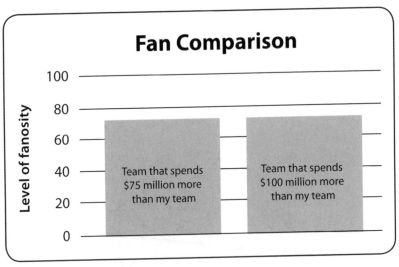

It was surprising to see that many fans across the country see both groups of fans as identical. This was not the case several years ago. Many people today ignore the fact that we are still different; to them, we are the same.

Take this quote from Thomas Boswell of the *Washington Post* in October 2007, on the low-payroll, talent-laden squads remaining in that year's playoffs:

"But except for the $143 million, buy-a-title Red Sox—who by now look so much like the Empire they claim to hate that they should consider switching to pinstripes—this October is going to be a tale about how less can be more."

In Boston, Boswell sees the same imperial warlords that embody the Steinbrenners' operation. Indeed, most baseball fans see people in New York and Boston as the same aggressive, overly passionate fanatics whose teams manage to suck their hopes and dreams out every summer thanks to their ridiculously exorbitant payrolls. They see fans who are loud and obnoxious, tossing around expletives that would offend their retired naval officer grandfather; they see teams who can't outthink other GMs, so they just outspend them; they see cities that create the "East Coast bias" of certain cable sports networks; and they see baseball as a sport for the major markets only. In other words, they think just the way Boston fans think about Yankees fans (with the exception of the caring too much part).

Martians and Uranians, however, know the difference. They know how one can tell them apart. For Martians, look at these signs to indicate without fail that the person to whom you are interacting is of Red Sox descent:

Top 10 Surefire Ways to Tell if Someone's Father Is from Mars
10. He has WEEI on speed dial.
9. He wakes up in the middle of the night screaming, "Way back, way back!"
8. Every alarm in the house is set to 7:05 PM.
7. All your pets are named either Papi or Youk.
6. His most formal shirt says something bad about Derek Jeter.
5. He's inquired about being buried in the center-field triangle after his death.
4. The very sight of pinstripes throws him into a rage.

3. He believes Tim Wakefield's Caberknuckle is a fine wine.
2. When Dustin Pedroia pulls a hamstring, so does he.
1. He does not allow you to disturb him in September and October.

And as a counterpoint, you can see there are various criteria in determining if a man is from the pinstriped planet:

Top 10 Surefire Ways to Tell if Someone's Father Is from Uranus
10. His grandfather clock chimes 27 times every hour.
9. He slams on the brakes every time the band Boston comes on the car radio.
8. He blames A-Rod for everything, including stalled subway cars.
7. His cell phone ringtone is John Sterling screaming "THEEEEEEEE YANKEEZ WIN!"
6. He owns a Mets cap tucked into the back of his closet.
5. He doesn't notice the stench on the 4 train.
4. Everything in his wardrobe features pinstripes.
3. He thinks $8 is reasonable for a small beer.
2. His wedding song was "Cotton Eyed Joe."
1. All his siblings are named either "Mick," "Scooter," or "Paul O'Neill."

In summary, Red Sox and Yankees fans are from two different planets metaphorically, and this book is here to highlight the differences so that you will be better versed and able to interact without consternation and animosity. Ultimately, we're dealing with two separate beings that share a lot of the same characteristics, including an annoying habit of making the playoffs most years and thus eliminating the chances for down-on-their-luck teams to win such as…well, most everyone else. Such is the cross born by Martians and Uranians.

Summary

It's interesting to see how the history of these two fan bases has taken shape. At first, Boston was the dominant faction and then, over time, the torch was passed to (or stolen by, no one can be quite sure) New York. And with the role reversal, feelings of animus between Martians and Uranians began to take shape.

One thing both sides have in common is that each is at the mercy of their genetics and hormones, which cause them to behave as erratically as a muffed fly ball during a pennant race would (though muffed fly balls do help to trigger said hormones).

Think About It

What is the main characteristic of Mars that equates the planet with Red Sox fans?

a. its rosy glow
b. the time it takes to orbit the sun as compared to the time between championships
c. its setting for many great movies
d. its swirling wind patterns

Yankees fans secrete brutoxin as a

a. defense mechanism
b. show of aggression
c. mating ritual
d. declaration of status

2

What Red Sox Fans Want and What Yankees Fans Need

It has been said that you can't always get what you want, but if you try real hard—and I mean *real* hard—you might find you get what you need.

We know what Martians and Uranians want. They want championships, among other desires that lean toward the distasteful and inconsiderate. But what do they *need*? What are their souls craving, and what do they require to subsist in this crazy, topsy-turvy world known as the AL East?

Emotionally, both sets of fans seek out different elements to satisfy themselves. For example, Red Sox fans were walking around in the desert, dying of thirst, for a long time prior to 2004. Yankees fans, in contrast, have been drinking for a long time (many are, in fact, drunk). They do not need water. They need something more. Much like the supervillain in a James Bond movie, they are rich and powerful, but need something to make life interesting again, so they do things like buy a weather machine in order to hold the world hostage or sign CC Sabathia, A.J. Burnett, and Mark Texiera in one off-season.

These desires leave fans from Boston unhappy while fans from the Bronx are still dissatisfied.

Want Versus Need

So what's the difference between want and need? Well, guys *want* a beer, but they *need* thirst-quenching liquid. Guys *want* a beach house, but they *need* a rudimentary shelter. Guys *want* Megan Fox, but…well, they *need* Megan Fox (no substitutes will do).

Before we fully explore the wants and needs of each planet's inhabitants, let's take a look at their present-day lives. We will be able to focus on what is important to each culture and why they value certain things more than others.

The Big Apple Today

Sitting under the watchful gaze of Lady Liberty, New York City is the most diverse place in the United State. It is crowded, expensive, and everything you get, you have to fight for—a seat on the subway, a parking space, the last cab heading to the airport on Christmas Eve, or a chocolate babka at the bakery. If you want to be alone, you have to get out of town…*way* out of town. If you sneeze in your apartment, your neighbor says, "Gesundheit!" Places with less-than-inspiring names like the 3-Star Diner and Ratso's still gather a steady stream of customers.

New York is not for the faint of heart nor the crummy of dress. Professionals navigate the city with ease and they look good while doing it. There's an efficiency in their daily routine that would make other people's heads spin. Pick up the subway here, transfer there, get off at this station, walk to that avenue, stop at this restaurant for a nosh, move further down the road to take a meeting, cross the street to use the gym assuming you remembered your running shoes and change of clothes, and then reverse gear to go back home and do it again the next day.

And the conveniences are unparalleled. You can get almost anything you want at any time of day. Hot dog vendors are in the streets,

> ## Testimonial
>
> My next-door neighbor is a Uranian and I'm a Martian. We once had a property dispute about whose land the shed I built was on. The fact that we come from opposite planets exacerbated what could have been handled happily and easily. Dr. Wasif helped us to work through our differences and found a solution to please us both: he suggested I talk to his mother, a real estate agent that found me a great three-bedroom Colonial across town.
>
> —Adam P., Hartford, CT

tongs in hand, all night long. Sleepwalkers can bring their dry cleaning in at 3:00 AM to avoid losing any time during their busy days. Bars stay open until 2:00 AM, and when they close, there are after-hour bars that stay open until the first ones are ready to reopen. There are bars that will do your dry cleaning for you. And dry cleaners who serve alcohol! Newspapers come out *before* the events happen, like in that old CBS television show, *Early Edition*. New Yorkers want things fast and they want them when they want them.

The same goes for their baseball championships. Yankees fans get tired of watching parades for every race, nationality, and sexual preference. They'd much rather be watching Derek Jeter on a parade float than gay and lesbian Tunisians blocking the FDR. Similarly, they lack the patience necessary to ever tolerate rebuilding. That means whoever the best free agent on the market is, they want him. If that guy doesn't work, find the next one. There's no room for failure…literally. I mean, do you know what kind of rent a landlord charges to house someone like Carl Pavano?

Beantown Today

Modern Boston is like New York if it was made of cotton and put in the dryer for too long: a "small" big city, with a quaint feel to match. The phrase "where everybody knows your name" isn't too far off the mark. You can walk from one part of the city to the other if you're feeling energetic, or simply take one of the five easy-to-follow subway lines, which are referred to by the letter *T*. If you prefer driving in your car, however, it might not be so easy. Whereas New York consists mainly of streets running north-south and east-west, Boston streets were designed by mental patients. And to make the situation worse, if you get the hang of one route today, it'll be blocked off tomorrow.

Boston can keep up with New York socially...until the sun goes down. Then it's past curfew. The city shuts down a little after midnight; the bars are closed, which is good since there's no more public transit either. On the plus side, if you want to go somewhere to be alone, you'll be able to find a tree in Boston Common that you won't have to share with other privacy seekers. Bostonians don't need the constant stimulation. (Ironic when you consider how many of them have the Red Sox on a Google news alert.)

This ability to wait for good things to happen (sometimes for generations) is not found amongst Yankees fans. Boston fans might have to endure times of frustration—like trying to drive through Chinatown—but with some hope and belief, the good times will show up eventually.

Value Systems

Because of their lifestyles and environments, each fan base is driven by specific goals, subtle as they may be. Knowing what each city presents its inhabitants will help us understand the primary goals of both Martians and Uranians and how environment has contributed to them.

Primary Goals

Mars	Uranus
Win a championship	Win many championships
Be liked/respected more than the Yankees	Be feared by everyone, even their grandmothers
Avoid a collapse	Rub things into Red Sox fans' faces
Stay ahead of the Yankees	Keep Red Sox fans speechless
Drink beer past the seventh inning	Make love to Derek Jeter

A common point of contention between Martians and Uranians revolves around the question "What is the difference between winning *a* championship and winning *many* championships?" To answer that question, you have to understand the value system adhered to on each planet.

Martian Value System

Fairness

Martians live in a more idealized world where everyone is given the same chance to win and in Darwinian fashion, only the strongest survive. That is by using their wit, perseverance, and in the right playoff situation, a shot of Jack Daniels. Any outside advantage, such as steroid use, is frowned upon. (Extenuating circumstances may temper this belief slightly, such as use of steroids by a Red Sox star.)

Red Sox fans were preaching fairness for decades before John Henry took over the team. But it was he who, after Alex Rodriguez was traded to the Yankees, sent this email to the press:

"There is really no other fair way to deal with a team that has gone so insanely far beyond the resources of other teams. It will suffice to say that we have a spending limit and the Yankees apparently don't."

Did John Henry follow the lead of his royal subjects by highlighting a need for fairness? Or did he have it in him all along to be the quintessential Red Sox fan? Either way, it's partly why Martians all like him and his straw hat so darn much.

Relatable Characters

Martians love their heroes, and Red Sox Nation has elevated David Ortiz to god status. That's partly because fans can relate to him (and not because all New Englanders are actually Dominicans living in exile).

For one, he has a nickname, as do most Bostonians. Most Red Sox fans don't know the real names of even their closest friends; they refer to everyone they know by nicknames like Mace, Spare Parts, Gabby, Tick, B-Man, Jack Rabbit, Downtown, Smitty, Dibbles, Ted, Hammerhead, and the Fribber (even Ted isn't actually that guy's real name). So Papi has an alias. Check.

Ortiz also isn't exactly a member of Jenny Craig. His BMI is off the charts for his height. That fits the profile of many New Englanders. Check.

He worked his way up from the bottom of the depth chart through hard work and dedication. (Whether he worked hard to learn how to

John Henry—former steel-driving man who could drive 15 miles compared to nine for the steam drill; current principal owner of the Boston Red Sox

hit an inside pitch or how to spike his protein shakes with foreign substances is something to be debated, but for the sake of this argument, let's go with the former.)

Fundamentals

Martians prefer the old-school way of doing things. You draft well, you develop players, you sign a free agent or two, and if you do so intelligently, with just a touch of luck (and perhaps tens of millions of dollars for a free agent or two), you will be successful. Ironically, that's the way the old Yankees used to do it back in the early days of their dominance.

Blue-Collar Workmanship

Trot Nixon said it best: "Like [A-Rod] says, he's running stairs at 6:00 in the morning while I'm sleeping and taking my kids to school. I'm like, well, I'm not a deadbeat dad, Alex." Ooooo, *burn.*

That was in early 2005 and it highlights the type of lunch-pail players Martians prefer to get behind. Bunch of Dirt Dogs, they are, not the stock market types we envision sitting in Yankee Stadium luxury boxes. That's why any Red Sox player born in the area gets the hometown treatment. That includes Jerry Remy, from the blue-collar bastion of Fall River, Massachusetts, the first "President of Red Sox Nation"

Dirt Dogs—the most true-blue fan of all Martians, this breed keeps track of outs, **KEY TERMS** assigns seats based on superstition, and doesn't change undergarments during a winning streak

Respect on Mars Means...

Not starting a "Yankees Suck" chant during a Bar Mitzvah

who has it in his contract that he must appear in every commercial on local television; "Framingham" Lou Merloni, who I think was from Fall River as well, a career utility infielder who has recently been logging hours on the very popular sports radio station WEEI; and, of course, the late, great Tony Conigliaro of Revere, who spent time in Fall River only sporadically.

The Game of Baseball Itself

Martians love to crow about how there needs to be a salary cap in order to save baseball and to ensure the level of parity seen in the NFL, which is now the No. 1 sport in this country (and also in every other country, except they play it with a soccer ball). It's an ironic stance to take since the Red Sox didn't win when every team was spending roughly the same amount, but one you can understand when you see the success the New England Patriots have had under a salary cap. Although now that there is a better farm system in place and better talent development than under previous administrations, it stands to reason that the Red Sox have a good chance to win with a smaller payroll...*maybe.*

Uranian Value System
Dominance

This is what it's all about for Yankees fans. It's not enough just to win; their team needs to dominate. At separate times in their history, they've won six out of eight, then 10 out of 16, and putting those times together makes 16 out of 27 World Series trophies. A legend is only so good if it destroys the competition. The St. Louis Cardinals are second on the list of championships and still haven't won as many World Series as the Yankees have *lost*. (You'd know this if you ever spent more than three minutes talking to a Yankees fan.)

Uranians talk incessantly about the '28 Yankees, the '98 Yankees, the 1961 home-run chase featuring two Yankees and nobody else, the '40s, and the '50s, and they use the word *dynasty* more than any other fans. (Well, perhaps not more than Lakers fans. The Lakers win one title and they break out the d-word, though I'm pretty sure they don't know what it means.)

Larger Than Life Characters

Yankees fans speak only in grandiose terms; rather than arguing that Derek Jeter is the *best* shortstop in the game today, they'll argue that Derek Jeter is the *greatest* shortstop in the game today.

What the heck is the difference, you ask? Greatness transcends ability. To Uranians, Jeter is larger than life both on and off the field. Most shortstops just play the field; Jeter not only excels on the field, but he's a bachelor you're jealous of (Martians call that code for someone who "plays for the other team"); he smells so good, they had to make a cologne from his odor; he wins championships; and he pitches products better than the other shortstops.

Plus, he has so many houses he's never sure which to claim on his tax returns. Now *that's* a larger than life character.

Respect on Uranus Means...
Paying the exorbitant $50 parking lot fee at Fenway Park

The End Result

Luxury tax? Phooey. Free-agent busts? Who cares. Treating other teams like your minor league affiliates? Fine. Depleted farm system? Doesn't matter. The only thing that *does* matter is winning championships. It doesn't matter if Uranians are going against 29 major league clubs or the intramural squads at the local chapter of the YMCA—if there's a trophy at the end of the road, they're happy.

Their Legacy

Where Yankees players lie in the annals of greatness is of great concern to Uranians. Other teams are happy to have one or two players they can claim as their own. Look at San Diego; Tony Gwynn gets inducted into the Hall of Fame and fans anoint him *Mister* Padre. The Yankees couldn't choose one particular Mister Yankee; they'd need a Lord Yankee, a Duke Yankee, a Keymaster Yankee, a President Yankee, an Admiral Yankee, a Chief Executive Officer Yankee, a Baron von Yankee, a His Majesty Yankee, a Troop Leader Yankee, etc.

Seeing Eye to Eyebrow

Given the discrepancies inherent in their value systems, it should come as no surprise that Martians and Uranians view historical events differently. To most baseball pundits, the history of baseball can be broken down into segments such as the Dead Ball Era, when batted balls would drop like beanbags, usually somewhere in the infield. Typical scores at that time were 0–0 or sometimes even lower. This era ended when Babe Ruth started smacking balls into the stands, thus laying the groundwork for souvenir balls to end up on eBay. There was also the Era of Free Agency, when owners no longer held deeds on players, which allowed stars to avoid spending their entire careers in places like Cleveland and

Dead Ball Era—a period of baseball from 1900 until 1919 when the sport challenged soccer's place as the most boring in the world. It's also known for being the most successful period in Red Sox history

Detroit. We are currently in the midst of the Steroid Era, when players grow to three times their normal sizes, all the while telling the public it was due to an all-natural organic protein powder that came from the sap of rare Panamanian trees located in the Brazilian rainforest.

However, most baseball historians aren't Yankees or Red Sox fans. Hence, the chronological categorizations on Mars and Uranus are decidedly dissimilar from each other:

How Martians Categorize Eras

1901–1918: The Golden Age of Baseball

1918–1994: The Great Depression

1994–2003: The Era of Exorbitant Salaries and Steroids

2004–present: The Renaissance

How Uranians Categorize Eras

1903–1922: The Pre–Real Baseball Era

1923–1965: The Golden Age of Baseball

1977–1981: Reggieball!

1981–1995: The Dead Ball Era

1996–2003: The Golden Age of Baseball (Reprise)

2004: (Baseball? There was no baseball played this year.)

2005–2008: The Steroid and Lousy Cheaters Era
2009–present: The Return of the Golden Age of Baseball

Martian Habits

So now that we have gone over our value systems, we see that, in a nutshell, Martians think statistics are important, whereas Uranians only care about one statistic: how many world championships they've won. (To a lesser degree, they think about the number of Hall of Famers they have to idolize.) Values like these lead to acquired behavior patterns, inclinations, if you will, that are inherent to one and, most of the time, not the other. First, let's examine several behaviors unique to Red Sox fans.

Quoting Statistics Accurately

Martians are intelligent in a baseball sense (and sometimes when trying to navigate Storrow Drive), though sometimes they do allow emotion to get in their way. For years, they had little else but statistics to fall back on. Statistics can help rebut any argument with Yankees fans. As Mark Twain once said, "There are lies, damn lies, and statistics."

I once had a Yankees fan sit in my office and ask me, "Why can't you respect the Yankees? They have more championships and more Hall of Famers than any other team."

I calmly said, "I do respect them, but the Giants and Cardinals franchises may feel you are not respecting them because they actually can claim more Hall of Famers than the Yankees can." (It would seem that 15 Yankees is a lot, but a cursory check of the baseball almanac would tell you the Cardinals currently have 16 and the Giants have 23.) Red Sox fans will always rely on statistics, while Yankees fans usually only break them out when the numbers support their case (even if those numbers are actually wrong).

Ask the Doctor

Q: Who was the more clutch postseason pitcher: Andy Pettitte or Curt Schilling?
A: It's not my place to comment on how much more clutch Curt Schilling obviously was. The prudent course is to respect both pitchers regardless of the performance-enhancing drugs Pettitte admitted to using during his career.

Keeping the Conversation Current

Why would a Red Sox fan speak of the past with a Yankees fan? One thing he certainly doesn't want to bring up is those few years between 1919 and 2003. It never ends well.

Accepting Failure/Looking to the Future

Martians may not like it, but they accept defeat and realize that losing is "part of the process." That is why the phrase "There's always next year" was invented not far from the marshes of the Fens. The odds of a manager being fired based on one lost season are minimal on Mars. On Uranus, conversely, anything less than a world championship results in a 3 percent citywide spike in unemployment once a Steinbrenner is through making "assessments."

Trying to Relate to Other Fans

It used to be easy for Martians to commiserate with Cubs fans. Now, Red Sox fans have begun to take them under their wings and counsel them. "You'll get there. Don't worry, we're saving a seat at the winner's table for you," they'll say. Cubs fans nod and smile, but they are thinking, *Why'd you leave us?*

Whining About Their Plight

"The Yankees outspent us again," "We can't catch a break with injuries," "The schedule makers gave us Detroit and the Yankees got Kansas City," and on and on and on. Hey, for better or for worse, whining is what Martians do, and they're pretty good at it.

Reliving the Experience

Forests full of trees have been destroyed in the service of giving Martians books that help them revisit their team's highs and lows. Every impossible dream, possible dream, probable dream, inconceivable dream, expected dream, nightmare dream, daydream, Gary Wright's hit song "Dreamweaver," dreams that come to us in a dream, and more have been put into book form. It's almost enough to make you want to stop buying those and start buying more copies of this one. Right?

For those less voracious readers (or illiterate ones), scores of TV specials and documentaries have also been produced. One HBO special examined "The Curse of the Bambino"; another looked at the "Reverse of the Curse of the Bambino." (Wouldn't a reversal of the "Curse of the Bambino" mean that Babe Ruth would be cursed? He'd be up in

KEY TERMS

"Curse of the Bambino"—a hoax perpetrated on the city of Boston by a couple of merry pranksters from Depression-era New York and kept alive by modern beat writers and columnists. It was finally revealed to be a farce in 2004, earning a hearty chuckle from all fans

heaven with no women and no alcohol, and he'd strike out constantly in sandlot games. That'd truly be the reversal.)

Exaggerating the Quality of Their Players

For several years, Red Sox fans believed Nomar Garciaparra was "the best shortstop in the game, hands down." Then he was traded away and became less than average…and wasn't even a shortstop anymore. Martians may now forget the heated exchanges with Yankees fans over who was the best shortstop in the AL, willfully ignoring the fact that A-Rod and Miguel Tejada were winning MVP trophies.

Waiting for the Other Shoe to Drop

The Red Sox have seen a 14.5-game lead disappear during the last two months of the season (1978). They've seen a one-game cushion and a two-run lead evaporate in the World Series (1986). They've seen a three-run lead get handed over to the other team (2003). There is no situation imaginable where Red Sox fans don't think, *This is great and everything, but when is something bad going to happen?* The other shoe is always out there, hanging tenuously over their heads. In 1986, the shoe was dropped by the Shea Stadium scoreboard operator who put "Congratulations World Series Champion Boston Red Sox" up on the board.

Martians envision each baseball season like a horse race that usually ends the same way, called by one of those old-school track announcers:

> The horses are being led into the gate. We're just about ready to start the 49th running of the AL East Stakes. Running nearest to the post is Luxury Tax Darling, the best horse money can buy. Next to him are Wicked Pissah, No Longer Devils, Maple Leaf, and on the outside, it's Rich Dumb Owner.
>
> There's the gun...and they're off!
>
> Maple Leaf gets out of the gate well. Wicked Pissah joins him at the lead. Luxury Tax Darling stumbles coming out of the gate. No Longer Devils shows a burst of speed to start. Rich Dumb Owner is still in the gate. They're switching jockeys now hoping that will help.
>
> Wicked Pissah pulls in front of Maple Leaf, with No Longer Devils two lengths behind. Luxury Tax Darlings is making up some ground now, but he's still far out of reach. Nearing the All-Star break, it's Wicked Pissah stretching it out to a 14.5-length lead. No Longer Devils, staying steady. Maple Leaf is fading, but here comes Luxury Tax Darling!

Past the trading deadline and toward the final turn, it's Wicked Pissah. No Longer Devils surprising everyone, but Luxury Tax Darling is coming up on the inside. No Longer Devils is fading back, and Luxury Tax Darling is closing fast. Wicked Pissah is getting reeled in. The lead is down to five lengths, now four lengths, after a huge burst from Luxury Tax Darling.

And *down* the stretch they come! Wicked Pissah and Luxury Tax Darling…but now it looks like Wicked Pissah is getting distracted. He's looking over his shoulder at Luxury Tax Darling and…oh, Wicked Pissah has just tripped over his own feet, and Luxury Tax Darling pulls ahead for the win! No Longer Devils crosses to show, followed by Maple Leaf. Rich Dumb Owner is still at the starting gate. He'll be heading for the glue factory.

Not Learning from Mistakes

In 2007, the Red Sox introduced a new second baseman named Dustin Pedroia. Standing all of 5'8" even in his elevator boots, Pedroia did not hit well at first, and by mid-May, Red Sox fans everywhere were calling for him not only to be demoted, but to be exiled from all of Major League Baseball. They never wanted to see or hear about him again. Six months later, Dustin took home the Rookie of the Year trophy, and Red Sox fans gave him nicknames usually reserved for George Thorogood's backing band and built shrines to him (albeit diminutive ones).

Of course, after Pedroia panned out, you'd think Martians would give the front office the benefit of the doubt the next time. However, when the team held onto Clay Buccholz instead of trading him for ace pitcher Roy Halladay in 2009, the fans once again questioned everything the front office was doing. Not that the front office is always right, but they didn't get put there because of family connections, so they must be doing *something* right.

Uranian Habits

Now that we can identify some of the behaviors commonly exhibited by Martians, let's take a look at their Uranian counterparts.

Jumping to Conclusions

The beginning of the season is a tricky time for Uranians. The Yankees get off to a bad start, their overpriced free-agent signings get booed, they fall a few games behind the Red Sox, and pretty soon all of New York is ready to start talking about football season.

Then, the Yankees make their inevitable run after the All-Star break. For some reason, every year, the Yankees don't start playing until the summer months. It certainly can make you think they are merely giving the Red Sox and their fans false hope on purpose. Don't put it past them.

Exaggerating Their Popularity

Uranians believe that with the cards stacked in their favor—considering baseball's salary structure and an ownership group of Vikings looking to pillage and plunder the weakest of their brethren—there's no rational reason that anyone should root for a team other than the Yankees. And that attitude comes straight from the top. On February 29, 2008, Hank N. Steinbrenner (the N. stands for "Nepotism") was quoted as saying, "Go anywhere in America and you won't see Red Sox hats and jackets, you'll see Yankee hats and jackets. This is a Yankee country. We're going to put the Yankees back on top and restore the universe to order."

Steinbrenner—from the German "stein" meaning "money," and "brenner," which means "spender"

Suffice to say, Uranians believe that deep down, all baseball fans are Yankees fans—they just might not realize it yet.

Obsessing Over History

We'll delve into this topic more later, but history is a Uranian's weapon of choice in any disagreement with another fan. The Yankees have won far more championships than their closest rival, so bragging about history and championships will be a constant habit for the rest of their lives and perhaps even their children's lives (but not their children's children, because I believe that children should not be having children). In this day and age, the Cardinals aren't going to catch up, and without a salary cap in place, the Yankees will always be contenders.

Yankees fans love to crow about their dominance more than any other fan base. Look at the winningest teams in other sports. As a matter of fact, the NBA's Boston Celtics have a better championship winning percentage than the Yankees; they've won 17 times, which is 27 percent of the total number of Larry O'Brien trophies awarded in the NBA's history. Similarly, the NHL's Montreal Canadiens have won 26 percent of all the Stanley Cups awarded, but you'll rarely hear their fans crowing about it. They might do it all the time, but they're up in Quebec so you'll never come in contact with them. The Yankees, meanwhile, are third at 25 percent of all World Series trophies awarded.

(Please note that yes, I've reverted back to my Martian heritage and am spouting statistics again. One thing every fan must learn is never to

Ask the Doctor

Q: A Uranian friend of mine told me you recommended Martians count to 27 when frustrated by Uranians. Is that true?

A: No. Though counting to get your blood pressure down is good, he's messing with you by using a number representative of their dominance. That's just childish and immature. The number of breaths I recommend is 2,004.

apologize for who you are. I'm sure any Yankees fans reading this book have already passed out by now anyway.)

Celebrating Prematurely

Uranians don't share Martians' fear about the other shoe dropping; in fact, most Yankees fans only wear one shoe to begin with, the heathens. They are notorious for planning victory parades and making playoff travel plans before Rosie O'Donnell (or any relatively famous fat lady) has started singing. If you were at Game 4 of the 2004 ALCS at Fenway Park, chances are you would've overheard one Yankees fan say to another, "Hey, Bobby, which World Series game do you want to go to, Game 2 or Game 6?" (As it turned out, they would've had an equally unhappy time at either game.)

Looking Down on Others

In the minds of Uranians, none of the other teams in Major League Baseball are really in the Yankees' league. Since teams like the Royals, Pirates, and Padres don't have nine-digit payrolls, they simply "don't want to win." It's a shame that other teams' fans have to sit through the losing, they say, but some owners refuse to spend the money necessary to compete even though the luxury tax dollars from teams like the Yankees and occasionally the Red Sox or Angels funnels cash down to them.

Many Yankees fans were, at one point, fans of other teams, but they didn't want to embrace the trials and tribulations that come with being a real fan. They just jumped onto the Yankees bandwagon and can't understand why others don't do the same. There's no judgment in that statement. It's just the way it is.

Ignoring Criticism

To be blunt, Yankees fans don't want to hear it. Don't blame your troubles on them, even if the cause of your troubles *is* them. Their team is simply playing within the framework of the rules and, in their opinion, they're doing it better than anyone. So they don't want to hear your complaints.

On the other hand, there are plenty of Uranians who pull a 180 when a New York team doesn't win…or when a Boston team does. For example, look no further than the Patriots' first Super Bowl run that was punctuated by the infamous "tuck rule" game against Oakland. Tom Brady and the Pats were awarded the ball back after fumbling it, but that was within the framework of the rules. Uranians often need to be reminded that "the framework" can be flawed—whether it be not having a salary cap or fumbling a ball only to have it ruled a forward pass. Criticize not, lest ye be criticized.

Giving Their Players No Room for Error

After he joined the Yankees, Randy Johnson was met by a nosy cameraman on the street and flashed some displeasure. Yankees fans put him on a short leash, and since he *only* won 17 games in each of his two seasons with the team, they ran him out of town on a rail.

A-Rod is in a similar boat. For the money they spent on him (then respent after the whole opting out of his contract fiasco), Uranians expect the world from him, and when he does anything short of otherworldly, they boo him with the fury of a million suns. Finally winning a World Series in 2009 might give him some immunity.

In fact, even when it's not his fault, they boo him.

A couple of years ago, a pop-up sailed to the left side of the infield. Rodriguez positioned himself under it as Derek Jeter moved in behind him. The ball landed between the two. Technically, that's a ball the fielder with the play in front of him should catch. Who knows who called off whom, but Jeter should not have been sneaking up behind his third baseman without calling him off. A fuzzy situation, but one that Yankees fans immediately took out on A-Rod, absolving Jeter of any guilt.

Looking Only at the Bottom Line

We've already touched upon this, but Uranians do not focus on how results were achieved, but rather what the results are. Others will criticize the Yankees for getting questionable calls in key playoff situations that have allowed them to win, buying all their players, winning with juiced-up players, and so on. But that's all immaterial to Yankees fans. The only thing that matters to them, again, is that they won, not *how* they won.

Walk a Mile in His Cleats

All of this information is a lot to absorb, but it certainly drives a stake into the heart of the notion that Mars and Uranus are the same.

Testimonial

I had never forgiven Yankees fans for the death of my father. It took personal, steady, one-on-one care from Dr. Wasif to finally understand that just because he died in 1978 does not mean Yankees fans were to blame.

—David Graves, Boston, MA

Now, does that mean that these behaviors are totally exclusive to each fan base? Of course not. Like women who lash out with fits of violence on *Big Brother* or *Dancing with the Real Housewives of the Apprentice* and men who cry with happiness when Victor marries Nikki for the eighth time on *The Young and the Restless*, each fan has a side that is prone to thinking like his or her counterpart. To better understand the other, you can nurture this side.

Put yourself in the other fan's cleats. For instance, Yankees fans have little use for sentimentality, evidenced by how quickly they forgot about old Yankee Stadium. The Red Sox, on the other hand, refuse to part with Fenway Park, for it stands as a reward all its own. (Of course, if it were up to Uranians, they'd stop by with the detonation kit at a moment's notice.)

If you're a Martian, spend some time thinking about what it would be like to have a new ballpark. It could be right in the Fenway area if you'd like. (The city doesn't really need a performing arts high school. That can come down.) Put whatever amenities you'd like in it. Make it a replica of the one you have now. Just get yourself accustomed to the idea that building a new one may not be so terrible. *Now* you're thinking like a Uranian.

Here are some other ways each fandom can get in touch with its better/worse half:

How to Nurture Your Inner Uranian

Admit you're part of what they hate

Ignore criticism, even when completely valid

Incorporate the number 27 into all daily activities

Speak loudly in libraries

Watch *Seinfeld*

How to Nurture Your Inner Martian

Keep a journal of the baseball season

Wear your sweatshirt and hat backward

Quote irrelevant stats when your team isn't winning

Talk about yourself like you're a small-market team

Watch *Cheers*

Gimme Gimme Gimme, I Need I Need I Need

So now we have a better handle on how to differentiate between Martians and Uranians. Fans paying close attention now understand that life on the two planets is quite different.

The trick is to use this knowledge when engaging the other side. It's not that Uranians want to focus on their past, but it's important to them. They *have* to. Likewise, when Martians point out the inequities of the league, even though they're roughly as iniquitous as Uranus, that behavior should be taken with a grain of salt.

As they begin to take into account what's needed and wanted, Red Sox fans can spend less time wanting what they don't need (a salary cap) and more time needing what they don't want (being lumped in with Yankees fans by the rest of the world).

Summary

Two different types of fans from two different planets, both Martians and Uranians are uniquely conditioned toward the way of life in their own cities.

New York, the largest city in the Empire State and the nation, consists of a loud and aggressive populace that demands what they want, when they want it.

Boston, meanwhile, is home to folks who bemoan the state of the game as they attempt to incite their brethren to take up arms against the Evil Empire. As their forefathers did more than two centuries ago, their goal is to bring forth a new nation, indivisible, under [insert your nondenominational higher being here], with liberty and justice for all.

But it all comes down to the prioritization of their goals. Martians really, really want a trophy, even more than they want another Kennedy in the Senate. But if they don't get it, they will survive as they have before for many, many years. Uranians, on the flip side, require the trophy. Yankees fans speak of "order being restored to the universe" when their team is victorious. Without it, their infrastructure and place in the world crumbles.

Think About It

What is not a top priority for Mars?

a. more competitive balance with the Yankees
b. a player that does all the "little things"
c. a spirited debate about why Don Mattingly belongs in the Hall of Fame
d. a hops-laden alcoholic beverage

If there were no World Series trophies to win, what would Uranians need to survive?

a. bragging rights
b. Joey Chestnut's competitive eating crown
c. the Red Sox relocating to Europe
d. annexing New Jersey

3

The Arguers and
the Arguing Types

They say the two things you should never bring up in conversation are religion and politics, but if you didn't bring them up in conversation, when would you talk about them? For some reason, people often don't include sports on the list of taboo subjects, even though sports are responsible for some of the fiercest metaphorical wars in our society. (In Boston, sports and religion are synonymous, so perhaps they've got it covered.)

Any conversation between a Martian and a Uranian is usually an argument waiting to happen. Sure, some conversations are quite pleasing: "Tough series coming up." "He's seeing the ball well these days." "Boy, that Mel Allen was something, huh?" It's not always that someone *wants* to spar. The conflict arises, again, simply because the two groups come from different planets.

Martians will shy away from any discussion involving the Uranians if the Red Sox are in the middle of a losing streak. Should New York get off to a slow start in the beginning of the season, their fans often play the "avoid talking until our team's doing better" card. Yankees fans always have the trump card of pointing out their illustrious history in the event a Red Sox fan wants to crow about Boston being in first place. It's a Uranian's favorite stall tactic; they've got nothing to gain by talking, only something to lose, so they'll just keep their mouths shut until things have turned around.

Anatomy of a Fight

So what are the necessary ingredients for a fight? How do they begin? How do they end? Note that we're not talking about flame wars on the Internet here—that's a whole other animal, one that can become as offensive and vulgar as you'd like since your name is obscured and no one can find you. You can say anything you want, no matter how outrageous, on Al Gore's Internet. But face to face, there's more of an unwritten code of conduct that one must follow. Of course, this does not take alcohol or a team's most recent losses into consideration; when those elements are involved, all bets are off.

Let's imagine a neutral, non-game setting. A fight in this situation is not the donnybrook you might find in the left-field grandstands during the sixth inning of a tight Red Sox–Yankees showdown during a pennant race. What I am speaking of here is simply a disagreement brought about by our misunderstanding the other's beliefs and viewpoints.

The Four Phases

Every interfanatical argument has four components. Each one is a separate and deliberate link in the chain, so let's examine each of them individually.

The Look

Upon introduction or visual recognition—perhaps from seeing a Yankees cap or the sloping forehead of a Uranian—Martians tend to position their feet in an open stance that allows for an easy getaway.

A sigh and a resigned slumping of the shoulders accompany their movement.

On the contrary, Uranians will approach and puff their chests out a little, taking dead aim at the Martian in their sights. (They don't aim a gun or anything like that…usually.) They're a little more welcoming to confrontation, as they have become accustomed to it in their city. The one thing that irks them is the mere *threat* of complaints that Martians use as their silver bullet.

When a Yankees fan sees a Red Sox fan, a smile comes over his face, his mouth watering at the prospect of dominating his foe. A Red Sox fan, conversely, sees his happiness turn to trepidation. He puts up force fields faster than Chewbacca on the Millennium Falcon.

The Condition

Whenever two fans meet for the first time, each is likely to quickly offer up his or her credentials as a die-hard fan. This phenomenon is particularly true of Red Sox and Yankees fans, and in those situations you can be sure that each will swear that his or her fanaticism has stood the test of time. For example, a Uranian can often be heard saying things like, "Yes, I'm a Yankees fan, but I'm a *true* fan. I was rooting for them back in the 1980s."

It's a technique right out of the used-car salesman's handbook: "I see you're wearing shoes. I love shoes, too. Since we're obviously

KEY TERMS

Interfanatical—involving two or more fan bases; the mixing of sports ideologies between fans with differing allegiances

Pink Hats—a breed of Red Sox fan new to the Nation. They wear crisp, new merchandise (not necessarily pink) without smudges or blemishes and believe fans are constantly booing Kevin Youkilis

KEY TERMS

cut from the same cloth, I want to get you the best deal possible on this car." This is all in hope of building a relationship, of finding some common ground; you're saying, "I'm a fan and you're a fan. We should have no problems here." Of course, problems will probably arise anyway, especially if the fan in question really *isn't* a hardcore fan and is, in fact, a bandwagon fan.

Red Sox fans are still fairly new to the fact that there are bandwagon fans in their camp. They are generally referred to as "Pink Hats," but since Boston had a generations-long championship drought, these fans are tolerated more often than not. In some ways, it's still 2004 in the hearts of all Martians, so everyone who was there at that time is considered a true, die-*hahd* Red Sox fan.

The Back and Forth

Let me preface this by saying that not all conversations end in a dispute. It is indeed possible for Martians and Uranians to enjoy a nonconfrontational experience. Should things start to get ugly, however, there are seven steps that can help you get through the entire ordeal. Let's look at these steps relative to a discussion I had in late 2001 with my best friend Chuck.

Polite Correction

Chuck: I read that Boston's payroll was actually higher than the Yankees' payroll this year.

Me: I don't know which article you're talking about, but I saw the figures and the Yankees had the higher payroll, as they always do.

Interpretation

Chuck: No, I read it somewhere.

Me: Perhaps the article didn't take into account all prorated salaries for players no longer on the team, or maybe it was an article from the beginning of the year before any roster moves were made.

Recitation of Facts

Chuck: It said the Red Sox had a higher salary.

Me: Looking it up online here, it says the Yankees were at $112 million and the Red Sox were at $109 million.

Repetition

Chuck: That's not true.

Me: $112 million is more than $109 million.

Automatic Contradiction

Chuck: No, that's not it.

Me: Yes, it is.

Incredulous Revelation

Chuck: No, I know what I read.

Me: I cannot believe you are this stubborn. Do you want a note from Commissioner Selig?

Severance

Chuck: You're the one that's stubborn.

Me: I can't talk to you if you don't want to hear the facts.

The Assault

When severance doesn't put enough distance between combatants—like when they're still close enough to throw things at each other—the final escalation is termed "the assault." When a Martian and Uranian reach this stage, the Department of Homeland Security usually changes the threat level to orange; things can get that bad.

The most extreme example came in May of 2008 when Uranian Ivonne Hernandez of Nashua, New Hampshire, was arrested for running down two Red Sox fans. The headline read, "Yankees Fan Commits Murder Outside N.H. Bar Shocking No One." The article stated that "Hernandez has been charged with one count of second-degree murder and one count of being an unreasonable Yankees fan, which, in New Hampshire, is a misdemeanor. She entered a plea of 'Boston Sucks!' and will be held without bail."

I could've helped her with a session or two of counseling, if only because it would've given me the opportunity to steal her keys. It was such a senseless waste of Red Sox life and over what, the smell of the concourse at each stadium?

Keeping that in mind, you will be interested to note that not all Yankees fans spew the same rhetoric and the same jargon. There are different archetypes. That goes similarly for Red Sox fans.

Testimonial

There are a million reasons why you shouldn't bother bridging the gap with Yankees fans. (Really, I've actually listed them. It took me 16 years.) But Dr. Wasif gave me the only reason I needed to appreciate the rivalry, which was also the first step in coexisting with them—you'll never get rid of them, so you better get used to them.

Theo E., Brookline, MA

Uranian Archetypes
The Time Traveler

He is stuck in the past. He so desperately clings to his "1918!" chant that it's quite sad, though not as sad as the rationale that goes along with it. The Time Traveler is the leading supporter of the movement that states Boston's recent championships don't count because players on the Red Sox tested positive for steroids that were found in their systems one year before the season they won the 2004 championship, a season when Major League Baseball had testing.

Or Major League Baseball wanted the Red Sox to win since Commissioner Bud Selig and Red Sox owner John Henry are such good pals.

Or the television networks rigged it to get great ratings.

Or Oprah Winfrey was behind it, since she owns the world.

This type of Uranian may also be a member of the "birther movement," people who don't believe Barack Obama was born in the United States and want to see his birth certificate (even though they've already seen it).

The One Who Ends All Discussions with "27"

Arguments with this type of fan don't last very long. TOWEADW27 loves those old classic video games Gauntlet and Asteroid because both had that button you could push to eliminate everything else on the screen. That's what "27" does for him; no matter how far into a conversation you are or how much you may be winning, he just presses that and poof! End of discussion.

Sometimes, they'll let you ramble on, allowing you to use statistics, historical records, quotes from firsthand sources, and video documentation before they finally turn off their iPod and say, "I'm sorry, I wasn't listening. 27 championships."

It can be very frustrating, I know.

The Baseball Fan

"Look, I'm a baseball fan."

This type of fan says this to differentiate himself from the fans who only like the Yankees when they win, don't know any of the players, and never go to games, yet claim the team as their own. These Uranians really love the sport and want it to regain its foothold as America's pastime.

Can you trust them? Trust is a crucial ingredient toward forging a peaceable relationship. Without trust, there is nothing. That being said, no.

Okay, I'm just kidding. What's a little relationship-counselor humor between friends? There are certainly Yankees fans who appreciate the game itself, can recite the starting lineups from the 1957 Milwaukee Braves (not to mention the fact that they know the Braves used to be in Milwaukee), and yes, they enjoy a spirited exchange once in a while with those pesky scamps from Boston. So you can trust them…just not with anything important.

The Phantom

This type of Uranian will gladly engage with you at any time…unless the Yankees lose. You might think that Martians can be prone to this type of behavior as well, but Red Sox fans can always be found and are ready to take their medicine. They might be numb, but they have grown hardened to heartache. It's one of the benefits of enduring such tragedy over the years. Like having an extra toe, it doesn't really come in handy and you may not like it, but it can't make things any worse. (Cleveland Indians fans have an extra toe as well.)

The Mobster

This type is, quite literally, a mobster. The team *is* based in New York, after all. What, did you not think that those guys sitting in booths at the back of Italian restaurants were baseball fans? Watching the Yankees just relaxes them after a hard day's whacking.

One thing to keep in mind is, these guys are always right. I mean, *always*. It doesn't matter how crazy their opinions are; just go with it. Below is a guide to handling even the wildest notion:

Mobster: "Not for nuttin', but that Jorge Posada is the fastest guy I've ever seen."

You: "Are you sure you're thinking of the right guy? It takes Posada 20 seconds to get to first base."

Mobster: "Maybe *you* are not thinking of the right guy. I said, 'Posada is the fastest.'"

You: "Huh?"

Mobster: [begins fiddling with his pinky ring]

You: "Oh, yeah! *That* Posada. He's like lightning. Boy, you sure do know your baseball players. You should have been a scout."

Mobster: "Yeah, that's what I thought."

Martian Archetypes
The Payrollologist

This is someone who automatically claims the Yankees spend so much more than any other team, it's irrelevant to even bother having a discussion with a Uranian. Any situation related to payroll causes a stir, but Boston's payroll is not the issue. Below is an example of this fan's mind-set:

Martian: Your team makes a mockery of the game.

Uranian: What about your team? They've got the second-highest payroll.

Martian: We only do it to keep up with you.

Uranian: Didn't you outspend everyone to sign Dice-K?

Martian: It's not our fault your signings can't win.

Uranian: We just did.

Martian: Sure, but you made a mockery of the game.

Or an alternative discussion:

Martian: Your team makes a mockery of the game.

Uranian: What about your team? They've got the second-highest payroll.

Martian: But we're closer to being the third-highest payroll than the first.

Uranian: You are to them what we are to you.

Martian: You're so way past us, it's not funny.

Uranian: We're both the same.

Martian: No, your team makes a mockery of the game.

This argument highlights the "circle of redundancy" that crops up in many exchanges between the two fan bases. The point-counterpoint just goes around and around.

Yes, the Martian's argument has some sound points. The Yankees are the first to point out when their payroll goes down from year to year, as it did from 2008 to 2009 when it went from the exorbitant $209 million to the bargain-basement $201 million. Instead of spending $72 million more than the Mets, they only spent $52 million more. Does that make it better? Not really. But they're not going to be swayed by the math; to them, it's about results, not specifics. (For the record, the Red Sox actually had the fourth-highest payroll in 2008 and 2009.

They've had the second-highest payroll only six of 12 years leading up to 2009.)

The Optimist

Whether he's looking toward the future or back toward the past, this fan angers a lot of people from both planets. He is truly the fan without a home.

On occasion, many of us lapse into this type of fan, especially when alcohol is involved. For example, while celebrating the Patriots' second championship in early 2004, I turned to a Martian next to me and said, "Hey, maybe this winning will rub off on the Red Sox." His euphoria transformed into contempt toward me and, after a pause that must've gone on for 10 seconds, he said, "I can't believe you just said that." Well, I can tell you I never did that again.

In conversations with Uranians, the Optimist will primarily look at the past with rose-colored glasses, saying things like "The Yankees almost choked there at the end of 1978, huh? They blew a three-game lead with only one week left to play to let the Red Sox get back into it and force that one-game playoff." The most famous example of this behavior came courtesy of former general manager Dan Duquette while making his case for keeping his job after John Henry's group purchased the team. Duquette said that under his watch, the "Red Sox spent more days in first place" than at any other time before him. Of course, that was the optimistic way of looking at it. The realistic way was to say he decimated the farm system and had no rings to show for it.

The Emboldened One

This fan is usually just asking for abuse. He might as well be hanging shoes up around his house waiting for them to fall after gloating about a modest Red Sox winning streak. Unfortunately, when the pendulum swings and gets all the way to the other side, it picks up an enormous amount of momentum on its way back to him.

Now, it's one thing to antagonize Uranians by wearing a Kate Hudson mask or perhaps even a Madonna mask, because the chances that this will come back to bite you in the butt are slim. (Dustin Pedroia doesn't seem like the Madonna type.) But to vehemently go after A-Rod for his steroid transgression shows a lack of foresight. I'm sure Martians didn't expect Papi to be caught with his hand in the "supplement" jar (Martians put him in the unimpeachable category), but you would think they might have reasoned that one of the names on baseball's infamous steroids list would be a Red Sox player.

The Negotiator

The things that come out of the mouths of Martians and Uranians can often be inflammatory, insightful, and intriguing, but they are usually subjective. That said, some things can still be seen as black or white, good or evil. The Negotiator will acknowledge an undeniable fact in exchange for agreement on a related point:

Uranian: "Fenway is full of thugs."

Martian: "I will acknowledge that, when that Red Sox fan reached over the right-field wall and took a swing at Gary Sheffield, it was uncalled for. But what about those Yankees fans that jumped into the net behind home plate? That's never happened at Fenway Park."

Uranian: "Well, yes, the fans at Yankee Stadium were stupid to jump into the net, and to steal Jim Rice's hat during a game, and to throw a knife at Wally Joyner, but Red Sox fans should not yell bad things about Jorge Posada's kid."

Martian: "Fine, that's out of line. But can we yell something at Posada about his ears?"

Uranian: "Deal."

Archetypes Common Among Both Martians and Uranians

The Manipulator

Taking bits of information out of context and molding them to fit your argument is an age-old practice here in America. It's very Fox Newsian.

A Martian once came to me and said he believed David Ortiz was innocent of using performance-enhancing drugs; if he was on the juice, the Martian reasoned, why was he so awful the first half of 2009? Obviously, he was neglecting the fact that Papi tested positive long before the 2009 season began.

Likewise, a Uranian who claims Derek Jeter is the greatest playoff hitter of all time because he has more hits than anyone else is simply manipulating the facts. Yes, Jeter does have more hits, but he has played during an era where not only is there an extra playoff series, but there's also an extra playoff team. So the chances for Jeter to reach the playoffs and play in more games have been greater than most of his predecessors.

(Okay, the Yankees won the division most of those years, but still.)

The Devolver

This fan allows any verbal exchange to devolve into name calling. Look up any message board: you'll find them logged on. Go to any ballgame or bar: there they are. They don't really want to argue. They don't have the mental capacity for it. Some common phrases you might hear include:

"Yankees win!"
"Yankees suck!"

"You suck!"

"No, *you* suck!"

"That's what your mother said to me last night."

"Oh, yeah, and *your* mother…"

Here are some useful phrases to use when confronted by a Devolver:

"Let's agree to disagree."

"You make a lot of good points."

"That is quite an interesting and unique way of looking at it."

"I believe I hear my mother/wife/parole officer calling."

"We shall see each other on the field of battle."

"When I first started talking to you, I thought you were crazy, but now…I'm going to get a bite to eat."

"Hey, at least we're not Pirates fans."

"Let us never speak of this again."

"Such is the nature of the beast."

Avoiding the Expected

Just because you're familiar now with the different types of arguing fans doesn't mean you will be able to avoid arguing with them altogether. Martians and Uranians are both bull-headed and opinionated. We certainly don't want anyone else telling us anything we don't want to hear.

I always tell my clients that although most disputes blur the line between right and wrong, each combatant can usually lay claim to offering some truths and untruths. However, in the case of a baseball argument, one (or both) of the parties may have gone *fahkahktah*, or

KEY TERMS

Fahkahktah—without reason or logic; screwy; backward; upside down; wicked retahdid; of, or relating to, any important decision Grady Little ever made for the Red Sox

in other words, batpoop insane. So be careful when you get involved with the arguments that are comparative, superlative, or hypothetical. These kinds of disagreements can go on for hours, days, and months at barbershops, schools, offices, and prisons, without any real conclusion or winner. Let's examine them briefly.

Comparative

In short, try to avoid taking any two or more of anything and comparing them. Favorite arguments between Martians and Uranians focus on Williams vs. DiMaggio , Fenway Park vs. Yankee Stadium (old and/or new), Nomar vs. Jeter (although that argument was laid to rest a long time ago), and Epstein vs. Cashman.

Comparisons are difficult to make because everything in baseball is relative. If Theo Epstein was in charge of the Yankees, perhaps they wouldn't have suffered a nine-year drought between titles. Epstein won twice with fewer dollars, but maybe Cashman could've done the same in Boston since he would've had the use of the supplement-fueled ManRam. Who knows?

Superlative

Trying to determine whose best is better is only asking for trouble. Rational baseball fans know it's impossible to judge whether Ted

Williams' greatest season was better than Joe DiMaggio's (answer: it was).

In 2005, *The Wall Street Journal* attempted to rank the dynasties of the major sports. They came up with mathematical equations and criteria that showed the Celtics of 1957–1969 had a higher "dynasty index" than the Yankees of 1947–1962. It sounds good, but there's still a lot of things to consider—you only need to retain seven to 10 men on a basketball team, while you need at least 14 great ones to win a World Series. How many teams were in each league? Does fewer teams competing make it easier or harder to win? How hard was it to sign good players? And so on. Superlative arguments are very tricky.

Hypothetical

If you just want to have fun and have a few hours (and hours and hours and hours) to kill, these are the arguments for you. Don't get too worked up during these discussions; as long as neither party takes it too seriously, a Martian and Uranian can spend an entire weekend series engaged in a good ol' hypothetical.

"What if Teddy Ballgame had been traded for Joltin' Joe?"

"What if the Red Sox had won one out of the two games they needed against the Yankees to win the 1949 pennant?"

"What if Boston's Bill Lee never had his shoulder separated? Does he help hold the Yankees off in 1978?"

"What if the Yankees never existed?" (It feels good to live in a hypothetical world for a while, doesn't it?)

Insanity-Enhancing Drugs

The issue of performance-enhancing drugs has become more prevalent lately, perhaps because Martians loved the fact that many Yankees were being outed as users. There was a backlash, however, after a couple of

Red Sox players, namely David Ortiz and Manuel Aristides Onelcida Ramírez (also known as "Manny"), were named. Now, Uranians have gone on the offensive, increasing the ludicrous standard exponentially in an effort to bust as many Red Sox as possible.

Speculating about how players can be on steroids is one thing, but recently Yankees fans have taken to calling into question Boston's recent championships…though not their own. One Uranian refrain commonly heard today is, "The Red Sox used steroids in 2003; therefore their trophies don't count." There are many things disregarded in this statement, though the Uranians' desire to revert back to a pre-2004 world is understandable.

If you choose to act as a negotiator in this debate, you might decide to debate the merits of asterisk-izing Boston's comeback in 2004. So how might one figure out which team benefitted more from the use of PEDs? We would have to recap some of the important moments of the series. Without having the chronology in front of me, let's use a typical series of events as an example.

Roger Clemens (steroid user) pitches the ball to Bill Mueller (non-user). Mueller pulls the ball to the right side where Giambi (steroid user) snags it with his bare hand. He squeezes the ball so hard, it breaks. Mueller is awarded first base and the home-plate umpire (non-steroid user) tosses Clemens a new ball, which Clemens promptly bites in half, earning him a warning from the umpire not to eat major league property.

Manny Ramirez (steroid user) steps to the dish. Clemens fires a ball over the plate but high and Ramirez takes offense to it. He starts pointing and yelling at Clemens; Clemens starts pointing and yelling back at him. A fan in the bleachers (drunkard, non-steroid user) starts yelling and pointing for the peanut vendor (steroid user) to toss him some nuts. The vendor throws it too hard and it hits the bleacher creature in the head, knocking him out.

Meanwhile, Bill Mueller steals second. Andy Pettitte (user) sees this and becomes so enraged, he charges in from the bullpen, thus igniting a bench-clearing brawl between users and non-users. Commissioner Bud Selig (user) awards the game to the Red Sox because he's friends with John Henry (non-user) and Senator George Mitchell (big steroid user), the one who created the report that named all the Yankees as users in the first place.

Hopefully, this chapter has helped you understand the different types of arguments and antagonists you are likely to encounter, and has given you a good idea of not only what to expect, but how to extricate yourself from them with your sanity intact. It's interesting to note that given all the history between the two teams, there are a handful of topics that continue to cause the most friction.

Say, that Mel Allen really was something, wasn't he?

KEY TERMS

Bleacher creature—any spectator in the cheap seats located at the furthest point from home plate who can simultaneously curse a player, drink a beer, and hit a beach ball

Senator George J. Mitchell—former senator and diplomat from Maine and current minority owner of the Boston Red Sox, he was named to head an investigation into the use of performance-enhancing drugs throughout baseball. The findings, released in his Mitchell Report, revealed 89 users, none of whom were on the Red Sox at the time

Summary

The bickering goes round and round like a Sit 'n Spin. With each argument comprised of four different phases, you pretty much know in which direction each one will go. Hence, you must be prepared. Just be careful when you feel yourself getting nauseated from all the spinning.

The topics are always the same, selected from a finite number of points, but not all are uniformly debated with the same level of emotion. It all depends on the arguer and on the arguee.

Think About It

Martians
Put these discussion topics in order from favorite to least favorite:
payroll
steroids users in relation to total championships
Derek Jeter
Yankee Stadium

Uranians
If you consistently bring up the Yankees' farm system as a counterargument to the notion that they buy their championships, you are most likely a:
a. nutbag
b. person who will end every argument with "27 championships!"
c. devolver
d. lawyer

4

The Psychology Behind the Hate

Centuries before Martians and Uranians were brought together, they were quite happy living in their separate worlds. Boston's fans of the Braves and New York's boys rooting at the Polo Grounds for the Giants never felt a dislike for each other. To this very day, you will rarely hear of any enmity between Atlantans and San Franciscans (though to be quite honest, I'm not sure they know their teams came from other cities).

When the Yankees landed in New York upon the addition of an American League squad in that city, Uranians and Martians attempted

KEY TERMS

Polo Grounds—a field once located in upper Manhattan across the river from Yankee Stadium, it provided a home for the Yankees from 1913 until 1922, but was mainly the home of the New York Giants. It was the spot of many legendary moments including "the Merkle game" and Bobby Thompson's "Shot Heard 'Round the World" and is where Yankees fans began to cultivate their obnoxious behavior

to engage in friendly competition. With the seed planted, years of cultivation had to occur before the flower of hate was ready to bloom.

Boston had already won every World Series ever played (one). New York wanted what Boston had, yet really had no means to get it. They tried to take it away, but to no avail. And any attention focused in New York was focused on the Giants anyway, who had all-time great Christy Matthewson on the hill and manager John McGraw in the dugout.

At the time, Uranians were not terribly distressed when Boston held off the Highlanders (the original name of the Yankees) for the pennant in 1904. Of course, it didn't help that the other New York team (the Giants) refused to play, thus preventing Boston from becoming the first team to repeat as champions. Collusion, you say? We'll never know.

It was several decades before any real animosity started to spark.

Inside the Mind

Okay, I know we weren't going to talk about any -ologies, but this one's important, I promise. It's the psychology of the fans. And to truly improve relations between Martians and Uranians, we do require a rudimentary knowledge of psychology, more specifically how to spell it. And since it's printed for you here, you're ready to begin.

The key point is that fans from Mars and those from Uranus are hardwired differently. Each is predisposed to behaviors specific to their own planet. They just can't help it. (At least, that's what the court-appointed attorneys tell them to say.)

The neurons firing inside the brains of Yankees fans and Red Sox fans both send similar signals—"chant 'root, root, root for the home team'"—but the motor functions of each results in a different behavior. One cheers and stands, while the other cheers and throws things.

The unique brains each species possesses create unique perceptions of the world around them, as well as opinions that they regard as facts. And while there is a lot of truth to some of these opinions, there is also a certain degree of mythmaking involved:

Martian Myths Propagated by Uranians
Martians drink beer through a sippy straw
Martians cry when watching "Feed the Children" commercials
Martians enjoy bird watching in their spare time
Martians drive mopeds or smart cars
Martians secretly wish they were Yankees fans

Uranian Myths Propagated by Martians
Uranians hate puppies
Uranians are the sole cause of climate change
Uranians are killing baseball (even Little League)
Uranians need to take off their socks to count higher than 10
The world would be better off without Uranians

Recognizing and identifying these popular myths can help each side formulate their approaches when forced to interact with one another.

Psychologists and Their Methods

For years and years, the finest minds in the world studied the actions and emotions of Martians and Uranians, trying to get a better understanding of what made them tick. They used a whole array of methods, including naturalistic observation, systematic assessments, and even a little experimentation.

During one trial, Martians and Uranians were hooked up to electrodes and shown videos of events while they were watched through one-way mirrors like lab rats. (Of course, they were given free beer, so no one was complaining.) An electrograph found that both sets of fans reacted to the same incidents, but their emotions were directly inverse.

Ironically, the only time both sets of fans had the same reaction was when YES network broadcaster Susan Waldman lost her voice. Other than that, they remained in direct opposition to one another.

This chart should not come as a surprise to you. It merely highlights the fact that we, as mentioned before, are hardwired to think differently. That's what psychology asks: Why do we not get along with fans of the other team? What causes us to act violently toward them? How many beers can your body handle before you make a fool of yourself with

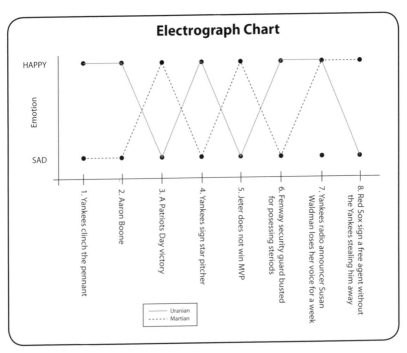

that waitress? What can our dreams tell us about our needs, wishes, and desires?

Even without all this testing, you can get a good sense of the psychotic…er, that is to say, psychological behavior just by observing Martians and Uranians in their natural habitat—the ballparks. (And you can save a lot of money that you can then waste on beer helmets.)

The Inkblot Tests

Another method of observation utilized inkblot tests. For those of you unfamiliar, Swiss psychologist Hermann Rorschach devised a brilliant way of getting inside someone's head by noting their answers to a series of inkblots. (Come to think of it, it's really a great scam.)

We administered the examinations at the Center of This and That next to the University of the Other Thing on both Red Sox fans and Yankees fans in 2007 shortly after the Red Sox won their second World Series in four years. The results were stunningly telling as to what these fans thought about.

The series of tests provided us with theories about how each individual fan approaches the world:

Silhouettes	Mars thinks	Uranus thinks
Ball going through Buckner's legs	tragedy	comedy
Big Papi's swing	Superman	Fat cheater
Fenway Park	heaven	city dump
Hat on fire	dangerous	fun
A-Rod knocking ball from glove	Bush league	clean play
baseball trophy	not the Yankees	ours
random ink blot	a unicorn riding over a cloud	an ink blot

Clearly, the inkblots offer great insight into the minds of these fans. These images could be interpreted a million different ways, and yet a high percentage of Martians see them exactly the same way, while Uranians see them another. As mentioned earlier, these fans have different needs and wants, which affect how they see the world. Yankees fans look at Red Sox fans with contempt, but it is not the same *kind* of contempt that Red Sox fans have for Yankees fans.

During a more extreme psychological experiment, we used B.F. Skinner's famous behavior box to observe how our subjects would respond under stressful conditions. The goal was to see if Martians and Uranians could find a way to live harmoniously together. In hindsight, the researchers deemed this was probably not the best idea.

Through their pinstriped goggles, Yankees fans see Red Sox fans as a bunch of unkempt, riot-inciting lowlifes.

Meanwhile, Martians see Uranians as the grade school bully who preys on those less fortunate and weaker than they are. They believe the New York fan uses force and intimidation tactics instead of intelligence to get their views across.

When the subjects were asked to turn the microscope upon themselves, their answers were surprisingly honest, though not always modest:

How Red Sox fans see the Red Sox

How Red Sox fans
see the Yankees

How Yankees fans
see the Red Sox

How Yankees fans see the Red Sox

How Red Sox fans see themselves

How Yankees fans see themselves

Uranians actually don't mind being seen as the bully. They are, in fact, part of the Evil Empire, a designation they are quite proud of. They wear it as a badge of honor. It means people fear them, which, as we learned before, is what they need.

Martians, on the other hand, are more averse to criticism and remain adamant that they haven't become like Yankees fans. They bristle at insinuations that they have. (And if you've ever seen a Red Sox fan bristle, it ain't pretty.) They are, they believe, the only ones who can take out the Evil Empire; call it their Luke Skywalker complex. The Red Sox are the only team capable of drawing as much media attention as the Yankees. According to a 2007 article in *USA Today*, the Red Sox attract more fans to road games than any other team, a statistic that must have Yankees fans seething with indifference.

Since 2003, the Red Sox have been the subject of some fascinating story lines. They lost the 2003 ALCS in epic fashion, made a failed bid for A-Rod only to see him land in New York, settled for Curt Schilling (who ended up pitching with his tendon stapled into place and helped the team come back from the largest deficit ever in a playoff series), won the World Series, lost their general manager who had to avoid the media by dressing as a gorilla, outbid the Yankees for a Japanese pitcher

KEY TERMS

Gyroball—a mysterious pitch invented in the Far East that spins like a bullet as opposed to typical pitches, making it difficult to judge the speed and trajectory of the pitch. It's a pitch Daisuke Matsuzaka throws regularly...or doesn't. Contrary to popular belief, it is not the practice of throwing a Greek pita sandwich like a baseball

that may or may not throw a "gyroball," won *another* World Series, traded their star slugger shortly before he was suspended for steroid use, then found out that two Fenway security guards were using steroids, one of whom was the son of their legendary broadcaster who wasn't in the booth at the time the story came out because he had cancer. Phew! And that was all on *one* Wednesday afternoon.

The Red Sox are basically like that guy on TV who prefers Dos Equis when he drinks beer:

They can sell out Fenway on a travel day.

They aren't deemed worthy of a story by ESPN. They deem ESPN worthy of their story.

It is said the .406 Club can direct wind patterns to dance the Macarena.

Legend has it that ships have entered the center-field triangle and never come out, yet somehow Jacoby Ellsbury always rematerializes.

Rats congregate inside the Green Monster just to get a look at their left fielder's butt.

News channels follow them twenty-*five*/seven.

Their walk-off home runs can feed the hungry in Africa for six months.

They play day-night doubleheaders at dusk.

The sun rises in the East...unless they are on a West Coast swing.

Newborn babies are named after their equipment manager.

They *are*...the most interesting team in the world.

So what is the psychology behind the hate? Is it simply that both teams want the championship crown? Certainly not, because the Pirates are also striving to win, yet they—hahahahahaha!—sorry, I almost made it through that sentence without cracking up. I'm kidding. We all know the Pirates are just looking to entertain their fans until the Steelers start playing football. But seriously, the Tigers are certainly vying for the same prize and there's no hatred there. And yes, I actually *type out* my laughter.

No, Martians hate Uranians because they refuse to play by the rules, and they feel that they can't compete with the rules laid down by Uranus. Conversely, Uranians hate Martians because they feel they are constantly being blamed *because* they aren't playing by Mars' rules. Both sides believe their rules are drastically different from one another; for example, Red Sox fans believe New York should only outspend Boston by 10 percent or so, while the Yankees think that margin should be much, much higher.

Martians are constantly blaming the Uranians for all of baseball's woes, and no one likes being blamed, not even O.J. Simpson. He went to great lengths to stop being blamed for killing his wife. (In the end, he kind of missed the blame, so he went on doing things he could be blamed for.)

One of the issues Martians can't seem to grasp is the Uranians' sense of entitlement. Those born to Uranian parents are born with silver spoons in their mouths; those born on the planet Mars are born with dirt in their diapers. This dichotomy has begun to change recently, but for decades, Red Sox fans believed their nobility was based in their willingness to die for every victory. They sweated, screamed, and prayed without ever knowing for sure if it would pay off. (Ironically, these other fans just came along in the 1990s, didn't have to work a lick, and—*poof!*—all of a sudden, they had more championships than they could shake their middle fingers at.)

So, is this sense of entitlement the Uranians' fault? No, not necessarily. Sure, it would be more of a challenge to grow up in New York and then renounce one's allegiance—thereby shunning your family and friends and risking ridicule beyond what you can fathom—to follow a more destitute team with no guarantee that you would ever be rewarded for your efforts. Sure, there's always that. But if you were given a team to root for like the Yankees, wouldn't you stick around just for a while?

And what if your family was so ingrained in Yankees culture that you were actually born with a birthmark shaped like Yogi Berra? It's like that movie where all the orphans are sitting around singing and then this wealthy guy comes looking to adopt one and chooses the cute red-haired girl named Annie, who everyone is jealous of because she gets to live in wealth while they live in squalor. (I think it's called *The Parent Trap*.)

Imagine you got to put yourself on a pickup basketball team. On one side are Kevin Garnett, LeBron James, Dwight Howard, and Dwyane Wade. On the other side is Mrs. Driftwood's fourth-grade Girl Scout troop, who, it should be noted, did sell the most cookies in the whole county. Most of us would go with Bron Bron.

That's how Uranus dodges blame here, by explaining their heritage:

> "My father was a Yankees fan."
> "I was born in New York City."
> "I have a medical condition that forces me to root for whoever's winning at the time."

These are unimpeachable excuses. If you were in their shoes, you would do the same thing...probably after using some of Dr. Scholl's odor eaters.

But Martians are jealous that Uranians were given all their riches, while not only do Martians have to agonize over each and every victory, they also have quite a deficit to overcome before Uranians would consider them equal. It just isn't fair. And as we mentioned before, Red Sox fans are all about fairness.

A Logical Compromise

I often encourage my clients from Uranus to take a more tempered view of their team's history. For millennials (anyone younger than nine years old), a World Series is not just a fantasy. Uranians love to crow about their team's success, their victorious history, and they all claim those wins as their own. They have 27 championships. But many of those fans arrived to the party after the feats were accomplished. There's not even any cake left with Mantle's picture on it.

Success is about the excitement of the win, the building of momentum, the explosion of euphoria, and the effort put forth resulting in the payoff. It's desire come to fruition. My solution is simple: each fan can brag only about championships for which he or she was alive. Those are the ones for which they put in the time and emotion. Even if they were

KEY TERMS

Millennials—the generation of youngsters born during the 21st century; those that have seen the Red Sox win more World Series than the Yankees too young to remember, if their parents dressed them in some kind of team spirit garb, they can claim it.

A championship is only as good as the memories attached to it. So that eliminates anything previous to your frame of reference, which should from here forward be filed under historical back story and not nostalgic experience.

Just check this championship brag-ometer to see how many championships you can acceptably claim:

Championship Brag-ometer

Year of Birth	# of Championships you can say you have
2001 or later	1
1997 or later	4
1991 or later	5
1973 or later	7
1960 or later	9
1930 or later	24

If you are older than 86, then you can certainly claim all 27 championships.

Oh, and the phrase "and counting" must be stricken from the Uranian vocabulary. Have you ever heard a Yankees fan say, "We have 27 championships…and counting"? And counting *what*? If they're still giving out trophies annually, then every team can use that phrase. The Cardinals have 10 championships "and counting," the Tigers have four championships "and counting," and the Astros have zero championships "and counting." It's superfluous. You don't need it. It is just used to annoy others. And if it's one thing I preach, it's taking baby steps toward a better relationship

If you're basing the phrase on what has happened previously, then that's inane. By that logic, the Celtics should've had around 30 championships by now; the Jets—who won one-third of every Super Bowl through Super Bowl III—would have about 12 trophies by now; and the Red Sox would win five times in the first 18 years of this century. It's silly to think past performance is any indicator of future results. (Of course, all bets are off if the Red Sox do *indeed* total five World Series victories in the first two decades of the 21st century.)

Understand that stripping off a Yankees fan's legacy takes away a vast amount of his identity. New York is still the most successful franchise in sports since 1994, but that happens to coincide both with the Steroid and Exorbitant Salary Eras, so take that with a grain of salt.

Now, I realize this falls into the Martian realm of fairness and Yankees fans aren't really into that, but this is a huge step in building a bridge of tolerance, and relieving some of the trouble burdening the relationship.

KEY TERMS

21st century—referring to the period of time beginning in 2001. The logic is thus: according to the Roman calendar, the time after Christ would begin on January 1, Year One. That refers to the first century A.D. and so exactly 2000 years later, we would reach the 21st century on January 1st, 2001...more than two months after the Yankees won the 2000 World Series

"true Yankees fan"—one who has been a fan of the Yankees through their "lean years" (1997–2008)

This idea is routinely met with a sneer and typically a mustard-covered pretzel in my face by Uranians, who do not find themselves in any position requiring a compromise. But what if Martians were to offer a compromise themselves? What does Mars need to give up in just such an equation?

Feeling Statements/Blaming Statements

As a show of compromise, I encourage Martians to make strides as well. The issue here is learning how to share feelings without the blame (and certainly not blaming your Uranian counterparts for anything a Steinbrenner does).

Try to share feelings without blame, as in these examples:

Instead of: "You guys are ruining baseball."

Use: "I feel frustrated trying to maintain a competitive balance with you."

Instead of: "Your players were all on steroids."

Use: "I feel disappointed that the situation got out of control."

Instead of: "You suck."

Use: "I feel hurt that our conversations have devolved into slurs."

Instead of: "You can't choose two teams, even if they both reside in your city."

Use: "I feel unlucky because I only have one team in my city."

The Victim Mentality

So as Martians despise Uranians for their pomposity, Uranians are constantly accusing the Red Sox fans of whining. And they have a point. Red Sox fans have adopted a victim mentality throughout their history. "Why me?" was their rallying cry for years. (As you know, Nancy Kerrigan is a huge Red Sox fan.) They've since loaned it to the Cubs.

The victim mentality is a state of mind that implies that if it wasn't for such and such, a person would and could be happy. Or in Scooby Doo-ese, "I would've gotten away with it too, if it weren't for you meddling kids and that dog."

In other words, if only the Yankees weren't constantly getting in the way of the Red Sox or constantly reminding them how great they were, then Martians would not have any problems. To think that this would cease all complaining from Boston is wrong. The Red Sox fans have a "whiney" personality, and there is really no point in trying to debunk that sterotype. They embrace it, much like the Yankees fans embrace their bullying personality.

In fact, Boston actually *honors* their biggest whiners with a "Whiney Award," courtesy of WEEI-AM. Every day at 5:50 PM, the voicemail box sings with a day's worth of callers who spout off about a player's mistake, a manager's move, a fan's rant, a mother's nurturing, an obnoxious sparrow's chirping, a movie's casting, a stopped-up-drain's gurgling, a teacher's teaching, a preacher's preaching, a leech's leeching, a beached

KEY TERMS

Whiney Award—given annually by WEEI to the Boston fan with the most creative and original complaint about anything along the local sports landscape

whale's beaching…I mean, whatever is on their mind. Boston is one whiney town.

Martian Identity Before and After 2004

Times are changing, feelings of entitlement fade a little more each day, and the victim mentality is reduced slightly as the two teams seem to be switching places to some degree. Each fan base is making over its identity. Uranus entered unfamiliar territory, going from powerhouse to upstart, unsure just exactly how to recapture that old glory.

Going into the 2009 playoffs, a Uranian was asked if he felt his team would win and return to the pinnacle of baseball. "It's hard, winning," he said succinctly. He's right. There's a lot of expectation. If you never knew what it was like to win, you wouldn't know what you would miss when you lost.

Identity plays a big role in determining how to act. The Martians' identity before 2004 was one of humility, of frustration. They were the ugly duckings. The question was always, "What would Red Sox fans be like if the team won the World Series?" And the word *if* kept them at bay. This took away the confidence of certainty. There could be belief (and *believe* was a word that Red Sox fans clung to), but outside of hope, no one ever knew for sure.

Then the duckling turned into a swan, sort of like that scene in *Grease* when the plain, inexperienced Olivia Newton-John blossoms into a babe that suddenly has men (or in this case, John Travolta) throwing themselves at her feet. The power is intoxicating. (I kid Barbarino.)

Martians went from fatalistic to optimistic. But Red Sox fans are never happy unless they're unhappy. It was an identity crisis. They won again and fewer people showed up at the parades. Cherishing every moment had begun to turn into taking it for granted.

How did this happen? How did Red Sox fans become so nonchalant about success? How did they take to treating Angels fans like second-class citizens, beating them at every turn, paying them no mind? How did the Red Sox start reminding the Yankees about the last time they won? Seeing Boston fans acting like Yankees fans was like the classic public service announcement where a father catches his son doing the wacky weed, the chronic, the doobie, the ganja (okay, I admit it, I Googled all those terms), and asks him, "Who taught you how to do this stuff?" And the son replies, "YOU! I learned it by watching you, okay?"

The Red Sox used to hate the Yankees. Before 2004, they stood in their way and they could never get by them. The Red Sox never had trouble getting by the Angels, though (uh, until 2009, that is). So the Red Sox, to the Angels, had become the Yankees. The only role model we had for dominating one opponent was the Yankees.

There's still a fear of the Yankees, but it's not that bad. Mike Mussina signed with the Yankees and the Red Sox had to outbid *themselves* to land Manny Ramirez. The Red Sox reserved an entire floor of rooms at the hotel where Jose Contreras had floated to on his raft out of Cuba, and it still wasn't enough to keep the Yankees away from him. But in 2007, they produced more money to earn the right to talk to Daisuke Matsuzaka. Then in 2008, the Yankees opened up Fort Steinbrenner to land CC Sabathia, A.J. Burnett, and Mark Texiera. And the Red Sox signed a 42-year-old pitcher coming off of major shoulder surgery and another guy with mitochondrial myopathy. These are situations that will always loom overhead.

Perhaps the Red Sox will not outbid themselves again, but they will always have to keep one eye on the Yankees who, not unlike a falcon, will swoop in at the last second to keep the unvigilant at bay. And unvigilant the Red Sox have been. They have toyed with overconfidence. It's as if they're saying, "We'll beat them with one arm tied behind our backs." (Which is pretty much how John Smoltz pitched with the Red Sox.)

But are the Red Sox letting the Yankees regain their footing on purpose? The chant that they grew up with, that they hated, that kept them as the good guys ("1918!") was gone forever. Don't you think if Superman killed Lex Luthor once and for all, he'd have a twinge of loneliness that even Lois couldn't quench?

The high school freshmen who used to be hazed by the seniors are seniors themselves now. And the old seniors are still seniors because they can't pass trigonometry and aren't allowed to graduate. Now you are on equal footing and have a chance to do something. It's the circle of life.

Summary

Martians and Uranians see everything differently. And that's fine. It's what makes them human (or subhuman as the case may dictate).

But any tension that arises from these differences may be quelled by attempting to feel instead of blame. This technique transfers the point of focus from the other person back to you.

The internal search for an identity and the shifting nature of those identities creates a lot of the problems between the two worlds.

Think About It
Which planet's millennials have witnessed more success from their teams in their lifetimes: Mars or Uranus?

5

Speaking Different Languages

When Martians first met Uranians, they were able to communicate verbally because, on the surface, it seemed like they were talking the same language. They spoke of innings and pitching rotations and pennant races. They were getting along fine. There were few miscommunications between the two planets.

But as the relationship evolved, it became clear that something was not quite uniform in the conversations. There were subtle differences, hard to pick up, that caused some initial confusion. To Martians, one word for one thing meant something else entirely to Uranians.

The two groups couldn't grasp what the other was saying. Uranians didn't know why Martians were being so dim. Stubbornness ruled these debates as both sides would wait for the other to figure it out and never made any effort to meet halfway. Pleasant discussions became more and more heated, which led to name calling and finally devolved into nothing but hand gestures.

It wasn't that one side was becoming increasingly dumb or pulling their best impression of Charley at the end of *Flowers for Algernon*; they just were using words in different contexts. That is, they were speaking different languages.

This fact is doubly amazing because their dialects were mostly the same, with hard, ear-piercing sounds coming out of their mouths on vowels, ones that could make coyotes howl. With more elaborate topics entering the environment such as championships, failures,

MVPs, salary caps, headhunting, and so on, problems in understanding quickly arose.

Lost in Translation

Languages are funny things. In one culture, a seemingly innocuous word might be the most offensive thing you could say in another culture, like the word *Bucky*. How could the same combination of letters become such a polarizing mirror of itself?

Before early humans began to speak, they just used grunts and growls. At least that's what the television shows filmed by Stone Age documentary crews depict. And then, over time, sounds and syllables began to get shaped into a series of words that could be used repeatedly to represent individual items, people, feelings, actions, and so on.

But the variety of these words is astounding. One culture looks at a spoon and says, "spoon," whereas another looks at it and says, "cuchara." "No, it's not a cuchara, it's a spoon." "Cuchara!" "Spoon!" "Cuchara!" And that's how the United States annexed Texas from Mexico. But I digress.

Similarly, Martians and Uranians look at the same thing and use different words. Developing a translation system will go a long way toward their continuing education in understanding each other, for some of the animosity stems from simple misunderstandings. What means one thing on Mars means something totally different in the barrooms on Uranus.

Most of what we talk about revolves around the topics of money ("Without a salary cap, the Yankees will always just buy what they want"), historical relevance ("The Yankees have a much richer history than the Red Sox"), and sex ("Screw you!" "No, screw *you!*").

When the two sides do speak in civil terms (or as civil as can be), they find a wall between each other making it difficult to understand exactly what the other is trying to get across. There is often a breakdown in communication because sometimes one person says something he or she doesn't really mean, and sometimes the other person hears only what he or she wants to hear.

For example, when a Uranian says, "Every Red Sox fan I know cannot name five players on their team," a Martian hears, "Why are you Red Sox fans so stupid?" What the Uranian meant was that "I once met someone that could not name 10 current players on the Red Sox," and the Martian was thinking, "There are plenty of Red Sox fans who can name the members of the team. You just haven't bothered to look."

When a Martian says, "I see that A.J. Burnett lost last night," a Uranian only hears, "I am obsessed with what the Yankees are doing." What the Martian meant was, "Burnett is an overpriced bust," while the Uranian is thinking, "You wish you had Burnett."

The Uranian language paints pictures in broad strokes. "Boston sucks," for example, encompasses the entire region, not just one particular person or thing in that region. They gravitate toward the grandiose. Remember that their stadium is bigger, their prices are higher, and their luxury boxes are more luxurious. You cannot expect them to be understated in any facet of their personalities. The same goes for their manner of speech.

Martians do not realize that Uranians lean toward the side of exaggeration. That's because Martians tend to take different liberties with their terms. They don't exaggerate; to the contrary, they prefer consolidating words in an effort to be efficient linguistically.

Translating Martian to Uranian

"Yankees suck!" = "Yankees fans are less than admirable."

It seems very basic to translate the sentence to mean that the "Yankees are not an adequate team and we are not impressed by them." But nothing could be further from the truth. Suppose the Yankees were actually toward the bottom of the standings for some inexplicable reason, like the Steinbrenners went crazy and started giving away All-Stars during their "Players for Clunkers" promotion to get inefficient gas guzzlers off the streets in order to save the environment. In that case, Martians would say, "The Yankees really *do* suck" and not the phrase you're used to hearing.

It's subtle, but you can see the difference. And Uranians, unaware of the necessary translation, react to what they think the meaning of the phrase is. They believe the word *suck* is (a) directed toward their team, and (b) a term describing their historical resume or recent level of play. It's unfortunate, because the Martians are trying to communicate feelings about their behavior with Uranians. Without the proper understanding, no progress will be made. Martians are trying to help Uranians (which Uranians don't want to hear anyway), but Uranians end up thinking Martians are more clueless than they initially believed.

"I don't understand how you believe our team sucks with its pedigree and championship trophies. If our team sucks, what does that say about yours?" is what Yankees fans are thinking. And any self-evaluation, at the request of Red Sox fans, will never come to pass.

"We have more sell-outs than you." = "We are better fans than you."

This is a Martian way of using a certain statistic to prove their fanliness. They use percentages rather than fan count; that is, that 100 percent of capacity is filled, even though their stadium seats almost 15,000 fewer fans than does Yankee Stadium. Uranians look more at the total number of fans per night. The fact that their stadium is vastly overbuilt for the number of fans that arrive to watch on any given night is irrelevant. That's not what depicts fanhood, and Uranians think Martians are childish to think it does.

Again, Mars looks at the literal translation of a sell-out. Uranus looks at the whole picture. Ten thousand more fans per night, some too big for just *one* seat, means a fan base larger than Boston's.

That's also childish. How many times have you seen New Yorkers leave games early? Or they disappear completely during the months of April and May. Neither has anything to do with the quality of fan.

"Your fans left early last night." = "Our fans are fans regardless of when they leave."

Martians like to keep track of this sort of thing. However, they only use it to undercut Uranians when it comes to talking about fan credentials.

On Mars, there are situations where fans may leave, but it does not diminish their standing as great fans. I've made mention of this type of fan in my previous bound work, *Red Sox University*. (In stores now. Ask for it by name.) There are Red Sox fans that are so deeply connected to the team, those with such an emotional attachment to

KEY TERMS

Fanhood—the state of being a fan; one's standing as a fan/supporter; traditional fanly qualities

Fanliness—the actions indicative of being a supporter of a specific team, sport, or player, such as painting your team's logo on your chest or pulling a fire alarm in the hotel of the visiting team the night before a big game

the team that they cannot bear to watch every second since so many seconds are filled with gut-wrenching developments. In Boston, these fans are called "Ostriches."

As far as Mars knows, no such fan exists on Uranus. Therefore, they believe any non-Boston fan who leaves a game early isn't a real fan.

"The Yankees buy championships." = "The Yankees attempt to buy championships."

The most popular argument, it's also the one that gets misconstrued the most. Every year, the Yankees spend exponentially more than any other team. In 2009 alone, when the New York Mets, with the second-highest payroll in the league, spent a whopping $149 million, the Yankees still spent 33 percent more than their crosstown rivals did.

Nevertheless, Uranians believe that Red Sox fans are just whining for whining's sake because you can't claim the Yankees are buying championships when they actually only have one to show for it this century. That's where the translation is needed.

No, the Yankees are not buying their championships when they're not winning them every year. But they are *attempting* to buy them. There's no escaping that fact. However, it's well within the rules of Major League Baseball, so everyone should probably take a deep breath and move on to the next topic.

Translating Uranian to Martian
"You just don't care enough to win." = "Your owner should spend more money."

Uranus has had it good for the past 35 years, ever since the name Steinbrenner entered its lexicon. Around the same time, free agency began and the Yankees have been able to buy whichever free agents they've wanted without salary repercussions. They just assume that's how it is everywhere. If owners are wealthy enough to buy professional baseball franchises, why can't they buy a measly ballplayer or two? Do they not think the reigning Cy Young Award winner is a savvy pickup? Are their scouts not qualified enough to make that judgment? Seems like a no-brainer to Uranians.

Again, this is where Martians cannot grasp what Uranians are saying, and Uranians don't say what they want to say in a language Martians can understand. Martians would like Uranians to put their statement into context. Although owners have a lot of money, there are myriad reasons they don't want to just throw it away on some ballplayers. Their baseball venture may not have the same budget as some of their other ventures. "Please take an introductory business course at your local community college," Martians implore to deaf ears. Again, they're just trying to help Uranus.

Uranians, in turn, are trying to reciprocate by telling them that all the high-priced stars New York signs can be theirs as well if their team just mortgages its future and doesn't expect to turn a profit for several decades.

"Your championships are tainted." = "Your championships don't count."

This is a relatively new phrase they've taken to using. Uranians believe that due to the suspected use of performance-enhancing drugs by Boston's superstars, the Red Sox didn't *legitimately* win any World Series. Martians acknowledge some validity to that, but only if Uranians feels the same way about New York's past and recent victories.

But the missed translation here actually comes in the emphasis. Uranus is not saying "All championships are tainted." They are saying, quite directly, "*Your* championships are tainted." That is, Boston's and Boston's alone.

This speaks to Uranians' needs to brag about their championship count and their desire to chant "1918!" again. Although Mars is making an effort to explain what the implications of that statement are, they once again realize that Uranus isn't looking for help, but rather speaking a different language.

Though you may always want to have your *Nation-to-Empire Dictionary* handy ($29.95 U.S.A., $35.95 Canada), here is a brief list of commonly used phrases that have different meanings to each planet.

Phrase	Red Sox	Yankees
Compete for a championship	Make the wild card and pray	Have the best record
He apologized	We're watching him closely	As long as he can help us win
Brief losing streak	Time to panic	Time to make trades
You suck	Your team sucks	You suck
You're wrong	Look it up	I don't care what the facts are
A salary cap	Spending limit	A cry for help
I don't care	This is killing me	I don't have to care
Rising young star	Future All-Star	Future Yankee
Free agent	Overpriced star	Future Yankee
Ex-Yankee	The enemy	Future HOFer
Johnny Damon	Traitor	Expendable
True fan	Baseball fan	Yankees fan
Fenway Park	Heaven	City dump
Rival	New York	We have none
Torre	Overrated	God

Other words, such as *choke*, cannot be described as easily. *Choke* is probably the closest any word comes to meaning the same thing in each language.

Another word that seems to garner much interest is *rivalry* and its root *rival*. It is an interesting one in the two languages of Martian and Uranian. It's been debated for decades as to whether or not Boston and New York could be considered rivals. There have been journalists theorizing that the Red Sox have been to the Yankees as much a rival as a nail is to a hammer. But that's more a humorous statement than anything well-reasoned. However, Uranians take it as something more accurate.

Martians use the literal definition while Uranians use something a little more figurative. It's true to form for a fan base that values specifics compared to one that looks at the overall picture.

The dictionary defines rivalry [noun] as:

1. the action, position, or relation of a rival; competition. Synonyms of the word are "opposition" and "jealousy"
2. a person who is competing for the same object or goal as another, or who tries to equal or outdo another

So you see that the relationship between the Yankees and Red Sox is the *definition* of a rivalry. There should be no question, but remember, that's according to the English translation and though Martians acknowledge that meaning as well, Uranians treat the following definition as proper:

1. when another can claim nearly as many championships as you. Antonyms of the word are "Red Sox" and "any other team in baseball"

"Red Sox are chokers." = "The Red Sox have a history of choking, hence can legitimately be labeled as chokers."

The Yankees choked in 2004. Are they chokers? The Red Sox choked several times in the past. Are they currently chokers? Interpretations seem to be liberal at best.

Do You See What I Am Saying?

Talking isn't always meant to be verbal. Without using words, Martians and Uranians still manage to misunderstand and misinterpret each other. Even the same nonverbal gestures mean different things to Mars and Uranus. It further complicates communications.

Waving

In New York, waving both hands over one's head means, "Yea! We are winning." In Boston, it means the same thing, but also has a secondary meaning, which is slang for, "Yea! We got out of these seats that we've been crammed into for hours. I didn't think we could do it."

Pointing at Head

This uniquely Martian gesture was made famous by former Red Sox player (and Yankees offspring) Pedro Martinez during the 2003 ALCS. Jorge Posada had been barking at Pedro for throwing at his Yankees teammates. Pedro pointed to his head. Posada and especially bench coach and resident gerbil Don Zimmer took offense to it.

On Mars, this gesture simply means, "Who does your hair? I would like to try your stylist someday." However, on Uranus, it's vastly different. It means, "I am going to throw this baseball at your head."

You can see how this misinterpretation caused the now infamous dustup during that series.

Testimonial

I was having nightmares about sitting at Yankee Stadium being tormented by Yankees fans. I couldn't sleep anymore. Dr. Wasif helped me to focus on less traumatic experiences from my past, like the time I had to give an oral presentation in high school, but forgot my pants.

—J.P. Ludd, Springfield, MA

Hand Cocked Back

In the dull roar of the Yankee Stadium crowd, it's sometimes hard to make out exactly what swear word is being used. So Uranians cock their hands back in the "ready" position. It's their way of saying, "I am going to throw this at you and you will be hit." It's not important what is *inside* their hands, whether it's a pretzel drizzled with mustard or a beer. The intent is always the same.

In Boston, the same gesture means, "I wonder how Wakefield holds that knuckleball of his. Is it like this?"

Hands in the Prayer Position

To Martians, this has the traditional meaning of "Oh Lord, please let us win." Since Uranians are not into prayer the way the Martians are, the only time they use this gesture is when they mean to say, "If I hold my hands real tight like this, I am less likely to put them around that Red Sox fan's throat."

The Middle Finger

By far the most popular hand gesture, this actually means the same thing in both languages and should not be directed toward children.

Why Mars Engages Uranus

With such a gap between what's said and what's understood, why does Mars even bother engaging Uranus in conversation to begin with?

Is it that they are trying to be accommodating, hospitable, friendly, welcoming, or anything that doesn't involve projectiles? Hardly. Red Sox fans would rather not make any effort to make Uranians feel comfortable. In fact, they prefer that Uranians conform to their customs while in their town.

With two stubborn fan bases squaring off against each other, why do Martians continue to focus so much of their energy on Uranians? Martians want to win, too. And not just on the field, for as we've discussed, it's going to take a long time to overtake New York's history. Martians want to win the battle of words. They want Uranians to start speaking their language. It would make things so much easier, as opposed to carrying around that Burlitz guidebook every time they go to a Yankees–Red Sox game.

Martians want to be able to tell Uranians that the Yankees should not spend so much on free agents, thus throwing off the competitive balance of the league, and they want Uranians to say, "Hey, you've got a point there. I'll run and tell Hank to knock it off." If that were to happen, Martians could mount their horses and ride slowly into the sunset having helped the village even though the village schoolteacher offered him a slice of her famous four-alarm pie to stick around a while. (Why it's called "four-alarm pie," we're a little scared to ask.)

Oh sure, there are times when Martians are stuck talking to Uranians, like if they work together, have mutual friends, are married to one another, and so on. In those cases, you can always get by with a tense smile and a nod. Heck, isn't that the foundation of almost every marriage?

Ask the Doctor

Q: I still harbor strong feelings of violence toward Martians. What should I do?

A: If you absolutely *must*, punch an Angels fan…though I don't condone it.

But Martians do still enjoy engaging Uranians in deep, philosophical discussions of great importance, like whether the '94 Yankees would have won the World Series had there not been a strike. Martians suggest not. (The answer is "no." Montreal was fixed to win.)

Why Uranus Engages Mars

Yankees fans are a willing participant in this little charade. They, too, want to leave Martians alone (or more accurately, want Martians to leave them alone), but they still stick around. Why? Uranians could just walk away and never look back again. Unlike Martians, they don't want to be proven right. Uranians *know* they're right (not bothering to hear the facts), so they don't need validation from any Red Sox fans.

There are plenty of other planets with whom Uranians could interact. They could develop a rapport with Toronto, but Canadians are so damn polite, it would make Uranians even sicker than they are when they're dealing with Martians.

No, the reason they won't look elsewhere is that the Martian language is closer to their own Uranian language than any other in the league. They can't communicate as well with anyone else, and really, why would they want to? Mars does a good tango with Uranus, something the Uranians are loath to admit. In fact, Uranians know that Martians will always be irked by something Uranians say. That comes from the familiarity they have with each other. Yankees fans know how to push Red Sox fans' buttons. For instance, here are some trigger words known to incite Martians:

Tainted	Mookie
The Bambino	Bucky
Clemens	Buckner
Boone	Zim
Frazee	Steinbrenner
Schiraldi	Damon

These are harmless words in Uranian, but among the most offensive you can say to a Martian. Conversely, there really aren't any words Red Sox fans use that get under the skin of Uranians. Just the fact that Martians dare to speak is enough to send Uranians up a wall.

As you can see, many of the problems between the two worlds stem from simply not grasping the languages. With the proper translations, some of these hurdles can be avoided and you can start your conversations on the right foot.

Different languages contain what seem to be subtle differences, but there are actually greater gaps than were originally evident. Take my recent trip to Spain, for example. While dining at a fine establishment, the bill came and I realized I had left my wallet back at the hotel. Using my best Spanish (adding an "a" to every word), I explained how "embarrassada" I was.

Well, amid the laughter from the waiter and the neighboring tables that overheard me, I found out that the word *embarazada* means "pregnant" in Spanish. Being able to learn the Martian and Uranian languages will mean fewer pregnant fans at the games, that's for sure.

Summary

A major factor in the consternation between fan bases is due to miscommunication, or more specifically, the misinterpretation of some key terms. What may be innocuous to one fan is the worst thing you can say to another.

The best way to avoid confusion is to learn the other world's language. Also, sign language can be used in certain situations where the noise levels are high and social politeness is thrown out the window.

Think About It

Martians
Just what do you mean by the word *buy*?

Uranians
What does the word *tainted* mean to you?

Taint, *choke*, and *rival* are three words that are easily misunderstood by both groups. Can you name any others that have not been mentioned?

6

Understanding Our Emotional Needs

Even after the reversal of fortunes in 2004, Martians continued to be on edge when dealing with their Uranian counterparts. They were still emotionally fraught after years of battle with Yankees fans.

A few months after the 2004 World Series, my friend Jeff (proudly wearing his Boston Red Sox 2004 Championship hat) and I found ourselves at a breakfast spot along the ocean in San Diego.

After placing his order (the fat-free yogurt and granola with a green tea smoothie—er, I mean Italian sausage and a large beer), the smug little clerk behind the counter said "1918."

As if a bell had been rung near Pavlov's dog, Jeff flew into a fit of rage, dismantling the countertop, tossing condiments everywhere, crumbling muffins, screaming, "We won the World Series! You think you can still taunt me with your childish little chants? You're not better than me! I'm your equal now, so you have to deal with it! Now go back to your videos of last century when you won and weep some more!"

That got the attention of the customers…and the manager, the cops outside, and the usually comatose burnouts on the beach. The clerk looked at my friend, speechless for several seconds, before clarifying in a barely audible, shaking voice, "Uh, your meal…it comes to 19 dollars and 18 cents, sir."

I caught Jeff's reflection in the napkin dispenser (from which all of its contents had been emptied) and I marked that moment down as the reddest his face had ever become. Reaching into his pocket, he pulled out $50 and handed it to the girl. "Keep the change," he said, mustering the best smile he could.

The sweet minimum-wage-earning teen was unprepared for his outburst, but was quite accepting of his apology as my friend was being led out of there in handcuffs. Still, it was not her fault, as she was neither from Mars nor Uranus, and didn't even know that we really existed.

In hindsight, my friend should've read the situation better. She was about 16 and living by the beach, with pigtails and a Henna tattoo of a dolphin on her shoulder. That's not exactly what Uranians look like or where Uranians hang out. After all the years he'd been around Yankees fans, he should have realized she was not the type to activate petty little trigger points for her own pleasure. She was just going to be behind the counter until the tide rolled in, then she'd be hanging 10 or 11, whatever her ilk does.

The point is, our emotions get the best of us sometimes. And Martians and Uranians are nothing if not emotional beings.

A Wide Range of Emotions

There's a fascinating display of the emotional spectrum that I'd like to show you, but instead will present to you Plutchik's Wheel of Emotions. (Feel free to don your nightcaps now.)

At first sight, it looks obvious that Plutchik was some hippie love child with way too much time on his hands, so he came up with this. Then we see the clear separation between each internal song that we can perform on a daily basis; a melody of highs and lows from bliss to despair, aggravation to panic.

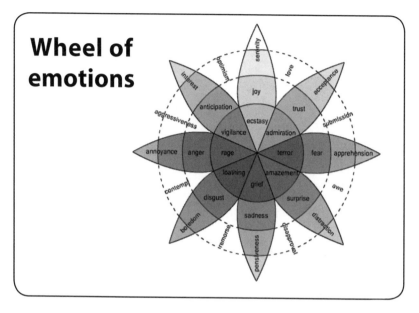

Wheel of emotions

We see that, though we touch upon all these emotions from time to time, some are decidedly more Martian while others are more Uranian. Generally speaking, anger and disgust are primarily a Uranian feeling. This does not mean that Martians are incapable of either anger or disgust. It just means that their makeup does not make them as pre-disposed to outbursts of anger or disgust. As I've proven, it can still be achieved. For Yankees fans, it's kind of like their fallback emotion. They're disgusted by the failures on the team, they're bored by the small-market teams that think they have a shot at beating them, they're disgusted when their team loses to those small-market teams, they're bored by the season leading up to the playoffs, and they *loathe* Red Sox fans.

Why is it that Uranians are so angry? Note the model. Anger is the polar opposite of fear. Fear is not a sentiment they express frequently. Yankees fans don't sit around worrying, "What if Rivera doesn't get the save this time?" or "What if Jeter doesn't come through in the clutch?"

They might think it, but they're not going to waste their time worrying or praying (those are Martian practices).

Hence, it is a greater stretch for Uranians to reach fear from their positions of anger and disgust. Red Sox fans live more comfortably with fear and therefore have a longer way to go in order to achieve aggression. They can get there, certainly, but it's not a place they're most comfortable.

Likewise, trust is not an issue Uranians deal with. They typically begin by distrusting their players: "I don't like this new free-agent pick-up. He's already lost a game for us, da bum!"

Advanced Emotions

Let's not get crazy and say Martians trust their team unconditionally, though. Emotionally, they are just more likely to do it because of an admiration they carry for their players. And admiration is different from love. Uranians certainly love their heroes and they can achieve admiration quite easily, but Boston is a different town. The players can go out after the games and find they're in a small city and everyone knows their names. Martians will buy them a drink and treat them like kings. That is, unless they're really sucking it up; then fans will leap right over to contempt.

But what of J.D. Drew? Can you really say Red Sox fans admire him? Well, disapproval is an advanced emotion, a combination of two adjoining basic emotions. Two emotions together bring up potent feelings that both sides can access equally. It's like putting Tobasco sauce with Habanero sauce. Ay, muy caliente, señor!

Martians admire things about him, but he hasn't reached full acceptance yet. He's closer to acceptance than disgust, though, which is a good start and a place where Edgar Renteria never got. He's near disapproval. Disapproval is one of those terms that is a combination of surprise and sadness; fans were surprised to see he couldn't perform as well as they had originally anticipated and they're sad about that.

It's in direct opposition to optimism. When a high-priced free agent is signed, you have to imagine he will bring with him the numbers that are expected of him. You do not yet want to fall into disappointment. Anticipation plus joy is how you come upon optimism, which is what the Yankees bought after signing A.J. Burnett, CC Sabathia, and Mark Texeira in the off-season. That makes Uranians confident, or optimistic, the team can win.

Will they love their newest Yankees? Perhaps, but they first have to bring fans joy, which is when the fans will show acceptance, for love is joy plus acceptance. The team's World Series victory in 2009 was a start.

Martians *love* the Red Sox. They bring them joy much of the time, but even in times of sadness, they accept what the Fates bring. Love is hard, especially when you have to play the Yankees all the time.

You'll notice from the wheel that Martians and Uranians spend much of their time near the inside, in the "danger zone of emotions." It is in this zone where extreme actions take place. There's showing interest and then there's vigilance. Martians are vigilant that Uranians don't gain any ground on them. Then there's boredom and then loathing. Uranians loathe Martians and vice versa. Winning a championship brings ecstasy. Apprehension is skipped over in favor of fear, sometimes terror, like when Grady Little kept Pedro Martinez in too long.

Why Martians Are Unhappy

Why are Red Sox fans unhappy? Well, first we must go back a ways to a little book I like to call "The Bible." The story of Cain and Abel is eerily similar to the story of Boston and New York (though Cain was a much better shortstop than Boston ever had).

KEY TERMS

Soxism—equal parts nationality, ethnicity, and religion, it refers to a set of beliefs adhered to by Red Sox Nation. Major tenets include singing "so good so good so good!" during "Sweet Caroline"; not celebrating before the final out; and speaking poorly about any Steinbrenner

It's a religious tale, but whether you study Soxism or Yankianity, you know the story well. Boston was given life by Commissioner Ban Johnson; New York was then birthed two years later as the younger sibling to Boston.

Cain, the elder, kills his brother Abel after growing jealous of him and God's favoritism toward him. The real motive was ambiguous and some scholars agree that it actually had to do with women. Cain and Abel were going to marry twins, and Cain wanted the hotter trophy wife, so to speak. But Abel got that babe, along with 26 other trophies.

The difference in the analogy to the biblical story is that, in the baseball version, Abel beat the living stuffing out of Cain every time he tried to get near one of those wives. That is, until recently.

Boston finally won the World Series. The Curse of the Bambino was ended. There was to be no more insecurity, no more heartache, and, most importantly, no more torment. Yet, there still is. Martians want to be held in the same regard as Yankees fans (though not when it comes to comparing the two, of course). They no longer want to be treated like second-class citizens, foolish for believing in their dreams. Both teams are winners, yet one side refuses to recognize that as an accomplishment on par with their own accomplishments.

The Yankees have always had players among the greatest of their generations. Ruth (thank you, Boston), Gehrig, DiMaggio, Mantle, Reggie, Goose (picked up at the retail store as one of the first free agents), and yes, even Mattingly. He was solid.

That brings us to the current age when Jeter, Posada, and Rivera have taken the Yankees to seven pennants and five championships. So yes, there is a demand for excellence. Anything less is unsatisfactory. Emotionally, Uranians need winning.

Aside from their first 20 years in the league, the Yankees have been to the World Series 45 percent of the time. For you people who have trouble with math out there, that's almost a quarter of them. (You're bad at math—what difference does it make what I tell you?)

Actually, there's a similarity to the Celtics in that regard. The Lakers, their archrival, had won five NBA crowns before the Celtics zoomed by them on the list. Then, facing a sizable deficit, the Lakers closed the gap a little. Now obviously, the Yankees have a bigger lead and the gap is still quite large, but the pacing of it is similar.

Besides comeuppance—and the destruction of the Yankees' entire infrastructure—what Martians want most is the recognition they deserve for what they meant to the Yankees and their dominance. The official numbers say the Yankees have won 27 championships and the

KEY TERMS

Yankianity—a branch of religion as equally zealous as Soxism. Its savior is believed to have placed a curse upon their rivals for many years. Their Holy Trinity is the shortstop, the closer, and the rich owner. Their creed is "greed is good."

Red Sox have won seven. But if you look more closely, you'll see that those numbers are skewed slightly.

The Yankees did not actually start winning championships until Harry Frazee started giving the Yankees players in exchange for cash to fund his little theater shows. It was an interesting story, really, how the Yankees came to prominence with the help of the Red Sox. See, the teams weren't always so rancorous toward one another, calling each other names and insulting their players. Imagine that New York was the only trading partner in the league. How would that go over today? Sure, they like to outbid us for our free agents, but they're not willing to give us anything in return these days.

A Transfer of Power

Red Sox owner and New York resident Harry Frazee enjoyed baseball, but he also had a thing for financing Broadway productions. During his entire tenure as owner Frazee had trouble with commissioner Ban Johnson. The commish didn't hand-pick Frazee as an owner unlike all of his "binkies" occupying the seats of power for the rest of the league, as well as Joseph Lanin and, before him, John Taylor, who were part of the Fenway Realty Trust that owned Fenway Park. Frazee was just an occupant there. He couldn't even get a decent parking space and had to park three "T" stops away on Boylston!

KEY TERMS

Harry Frazee—former Red Sox owner and theater producer, he is generally credited with helping the Yankees begin their run of dominance, much to the dismay of fans of his own team

Frazee finally settled with Lanin, but realized he needed more cash so he got a large loan from Yankees owner Colonel Jacob Ruppert, who simply asked Frazee for his soul as collateral.

Around the same time, Frazee's ballclub was winning another World Series (his second) under the steady leadership of Ed Barrow, both his on-field manager and front office general manager. However, his players were becoming increasingly harder to handle, including rogues Carl Mays and George Ruth.

Frazee let Mays go, but he had a bigger problem on his hands with Ruth. He was a superstar in the making and Frazee didn't want to let him go. At first, he paid Ruth a nice bonus, even though he didn't need to. When he tried it again, Ruth wanted more. He was going to do whatever he wanted.

After the 1919 season, which ended with the outfielder/pitcher AWOL, Frazee decided he had to trade him. But to whom? Commissioner Ban Johnson had basically threatened every other team not to trade with the Red Sox. That left the World Series runner-up White Sox and the perpetually cellar-dwelling Yankees.

So the cash-strapped, frustrated, at-the-end-of-his-rope owner made a deal to trade George "Babe" Ruth, his superstar, to the Chicago White Sox for "Shoeless" Joe Jackson, the superstar on the White Sox. (It actually would've saved Frazee even more money because he didn't have to supply Jackson with footwear.)

The only problem was Jackson had just been suspended for life for allegedly throwing the previous World Series to the Cincinnati Reds. Signing him to a long-term deal just didn't make as much sense.

That left the Yankees as the sole remaining trade partner. With but one team remaining to deal with, Frazee called in his trusted right-hand man, Ed "the Backstabber" Barrow, to confer with him. (Not that

Barrow had a reputation for double-crossing anyone. He actually gave himself that nickname.)

A memoir found years later shows the two had the following conversation:

> "Conversations between Ed Barrow and Harry Frazee"
> December 1919
> INT. Frazee's Office
> *Harry Frazee, the much-maligned owner of the Boston Red Sox, stands behind his desk looking out over the city. Even with two championship trophies in his tiny office, he has the look of a failure. Ed Barrow was his field manager and general manager, his #2, the man behind the man.*
> *There is a KNOCK on the door.*
> FRAZEE
> Come in, Ed. Shut the door.
> *Ed ENTERS, carrying a suitcase.*
> BARROW
> This sounds urgent, Harry. What's up?
> FRAZEE
> Well, I just don't know what to do about—say, why the suitcase?
> BARROW
> (pause) No reason.
> *Barrow checks his pocket watch. He seems preoccupied.*
> FRAZEE
> I just don't know what to do about Ruth. He's out of control. I gave him a bonus last year. I gave him a bonus this year. He comes and goes as he pleases. I set up a breakfast

meeting with him; he ate the last waffle off my plate and left without talking.

BARROW

We don't have a lot of options.

FRAZEE

No, we don't. Commissioner Johnson has forbidden most teams from dealing with us. I can only talk to the Chicago White Sox and the New York Yankees.

BARROW

The Yankees? Go on.

FRAZEE

I had a deal in place to get Shoeless Joe from Chicago, but after that little scandal thing, it's off.

BARROW

(smiling) So you're stuck with New York.

FRAZEE

Yes, I'm—say, why is there a Yankees sticker on your suitcase?

BARROW

Huh? Oh, uh, damn vandals. Must've stuck it there when I put it down.

FRAZEE

Ah. As I was saying, my options are down to one. Does New York have anyone that you'd want in return?

BARROW

For Ruth? Oh, he's nothing but trouble. The Yankees don't really have any players I'd want.

FRAZEE

None? How about Bob Shawkey? He went 20-11 with a 2.72 ERA this past year.

BARROW

What would I need with another pitcher?

FRAZEE

Okay, do you like Frank Baker or Ping Bodie? Ping's an okay hitter and I think we can really market a player named "Ping."

BARROW

Hey, you know what? I just had an idea. You should make them pay you cash for Ruth.

FRAZEE

Cash?

BARROW

Oh, sure. Really stick it to them. That'll probably bankrupt them. And you can use the money to pay off your loan. It'll probably hamstring their new general manager into making any good deals.

FRAZEE

They're getting a new general manager?

BARROW

Hey, is that painting new?

FRAZEE

No, it's been there since I moved in. You've seen it many times.

BARROW

My mistake. So, listen, what say we call good ol' Ruppert and Huston up and get them to give up the goods?

FRAZEE

And you don't want any players?

BARROW

None of their players, no. I just want the players I have now.

FRAZEE

Except Ruth.

BARROW

What? Oh, yeah, except Ruth. (backing toward the door) Of course.

FRAZEE

Ed?

BARROW

Yes, Harry.

FRAZEE

Are you sure you're all right? You've been acting strangely lately.

BARROW

Oh, yeah, definitely. I'm just so happy to be getting Ruth. I mean, to be getting *rid of* Ruth. Did I say *getting*? I meant *rid*. Heh heh. Honest mistake. I meant—hey, hey! (looks at his wrist, which is bare) Would you look at the time? Okay, gotta run. Got a train to catch. See ya.

Barrow apparently told Frazee that he didn't want any players from New York...then became the Yankees' general manager a year later. And slowly, over the next few years, he began switching teams. He took some Red Sox players and dressed them in pinstripes, and put some Yankees into the red and blue of Boston. Eventually, Barrow had almost as many players from his old team as he had players from his new team.

By the time the Yankees finally started winning in 1923 (after losing in the World Series the previous two years), they had 11 former Red Sox players on their team.

KEY TERMS

Ed Barrow—former manager who took the Red Sox to the 1918 World Series, then took the Red Sox players over to the Yankees where he proceeded to preside over 14 pennants between 1921 and 1945

Knowing this, it makes the championship count both misleading and inaccurate, technically. Let's look at this more closely: New York has been credited with 27 championships, but the first four of those came with former Red Sox players leading the way. Sure, they had added Lou Gehrig by the time 1928 came along, but honestly, what good could he have been? He played *constantly*. The guy was exhausted, and probably slept while standing up at first base.

So a case can be made that the *Red Sox* won those championships, they were just wearing Yankees uniforms at the time. That's four fewer for New York and four more for Boston.

We must also remember that in 1904 Boston won the American League crown by narrowly beating out the Highlanders. They earned the right to face the National League champion New York Giants. However, when the Red Sox showed up to play, the Giants weren't there. Owner John T. Bush refused to allow his team to play the Red Sox. What's the matter, Colonel Sanders? Chicken? [Note: The author would like to apologize to the readers for openly mocking a guy who's been dead for almost a century. It was uncalled for and will never happen again.]

It seems Bush was worried that his team's opponent would be the new team from the upstart American League, the crosstown rival Highlanders. And he was worried about sharing the spotlight with another New York team. Waaaahh! Waaaaahh! Does baby want his wittle bottle? [Note: The author would like to further apologize to the reader for lying to you in the previous note. He swears it will not happen again.]

Any way you look at it, that's a forfeit. And in a forfeit, the crown goes to the other team, which would be Boston. So suck on it, Bushy! [Note: The author really has no excuse for that one.]

That means we add another one to Boston's total, bringing it to 12.

So the actual total number of championships for the Yankees is 23, and for Boston, it's 12. That's a little easier to fathom, and perhaps someday, to overcome.

I try to explain this to my Uranian clients, but again, they look at me like I have two heads. The very notion is something that Yankees fans can't handle emotionally because it would mean they were closer to the pack than they thought, even though it would take one heck of a run to catch them. Still, Boston would be within the ballpark.

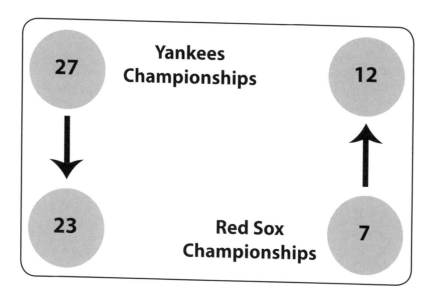

It's a good thing Boston knows better than to relive the actions of the Frazee era. Imagine trading away their high-priced superstar slugger simply because he was a problem in the clubhouse and only played whenever he felt like it. It's not like the Red Sox would ever trade away a guy like Manny Ramir...uh, scratch that thought.

Ironically, Barrow built his championship teams through relatively few high-priced purchases and developed talent through what was called a "farm system" because they treated those players like cattle. In the years they were winning and Boston was mired in incompetence, the Red Sox, under Tom Yawkey's ownership, had a higher payroll than New York did. Go figure. Fast-forward to today where Boston has been the team with the lower payroll, but once they finally started building from within, they have become arguably more successful than the Yankees. Again, go figure.

Why Uranus Is Dissatisfied

You might ask, what do Uranians have to be dissatisfied about? Once they get past the fact that they have to mortgage their homes to take in a ballgame, it's all pretty much sunshine and puppy dogs. It's nothing like being a Nationals fan, which is more along the lines of monsoons and rabid pit bulls.

Let me explain it this way—when you used to eat lobster and now you're eating clams, you'd be unhappy, too. Uranians had it all. They got used to that life. We're talking a fan base who celebrated 16 championships in 27 years. That's not even a challenge. Other teams had to throw up their hands before the season even started. The Red Sox tried to do this, but they botched that too, waiting until the last few weeks of the season to give in.

The New York Yankees are not usually acknowledged as working hard to achieve their place in the baseball hierarchy. As we mentioned in

Ask the Doctor

Q: As a Uranian, if I'm around Red Sox and Phillies fans, with whom should I side?

A: It's natural to want to side with a Phillies fan, as there's no real rivalry there. However, that notion goes out the window when football season rolls around. I suggest showing your brotherhood with your Martian brothers in this situation. It promotes trust and there's nothing wrong with extending an olive branch once in a while, which is really the main tenet I preach.

Chapter 4, others perceive the Yankees as a team that simply outspends everyone else in order to get the best talent. But when the Yankees win, it's generally with a core of their own homegrown guys, surrounded by high-priced mercenaries. They have top-notch player development and harbor resentment toward those that say they buy all their championships. As we learned in the last chapter, they can't be buying their championships if they aren't winning every year.

However, let's not get wacky here. I mean, they're not Minnesota. They do supplement their younger stars with outsiders—very, very high-priced outsiders. But that's how you build a team. There's nothing wrong with that, as long as the system remains the same. It just so happens that they are able to outspend all other teams to get the highest-end, top-shelf players on the market, as well as to re-sign their own stars. They're at Saks Fifth Avenue while the Toronto Blue Jays general manager is at The Gap...or the French Canadian version of it, Le Gap.

Yankees fans demand the best. Red Sox fans hope they get someone who can do the job and many times, that's whoever has been left over by the Yankees. Carl Pavano visited Boston and signed with the Yankees, so Boston went out and got Matt Clement. Boy, didn't that turn out great for both clubs?

Schadenfreude

As we know, Yankees fans need to be able to crow about champion-ships. It's in their DNA (dominant narcissistic attitude). And they're confident that, in their lifetimes, they'll never have to worry about any team approaching their dominance. It's safe to believe that since there are really only 10 teams that are able to contend each season, given the current financial situation.

However, the New York Yankees went almost a decade without winning another title, which left their fans feeling empty and lacking what they need. Without increasing their lead in the number of cham-pionships, they attempted to do the next best thing—cheat the Red Sox out of theirs, thereby increasing their lead in the tally.

Such is the nature of *schadenfreude*. This is pleasure derived from the misfortune of others and not a Bavarian pastry, as many believe. When there's no chance to "root, root, root for the home team," why not turn your energies toward rooting *against* your rival? That is the gist of the popular shirts emblazoned with the words "I root for two teams: The Red Sox and whoever is playing the Yankees" (or the converse of it for Uranians).

And that's why a prevalent foray of verbiage being slung today between Martians and Uranians centers on the subject of tainted

KEY TERMS

Schadenfreude—a German word meaning "pleasure derived from the misfortune of others," it is a major force in the Mars/Uranus relationship

championships, primarily those of a World Series variety and not the annual summer bocce ones where I swear my great Uncle Hiram cheats terribly.

The fans in favor of taking away the trophies seem to come from New York, whilst those that believe recent revelations change nothing are from Hartford and points east.

To Uranians, whatever it takes to deprive the Red Sox of what the Yankees want, but haven't been able to get in abundance recently, is fair game. They make the point that since there were Red Sox players who were allegedly on performance-enhancing drugs, the team must forfeit its victories. And Martians counter that if it were the case, then the Yankees should return their hardware as well. (By the way, how would such an agreement work anyway? It's not like someone is going to be nominated to go to Yankee Stadium, knock on the door, and say, "Hey, yeah, my name's Sully. Look, I gotta pick up the 1998 World Series trophy from Hank Steinbrenner. He should be expecting me.")

And Yankees fans, ever ready for a battle, respond in kind: "The Yankees who were found guilty of steroids were not the heart of the team. Bernie Williams, Derek Jeter, Jorge Posada, Mariano Rivera, Paul O'Neill—they were all as pure as the driven snow."

And Martians will go in one of two directions: they will bring up the names Roger Clemens and Andy Pettitte, both admitted steroid users (even though Clemens' admission is more of a roundabout admission because the more he denies it, the more obvious it looks like he's guilty), or they will say that those core players may not have been *caught* doing steroids.

At that point, one of the two parties will walk away. Still, things have become much more civilized in these sorts of discussions. (Back in the 1600s, ballplayers were burned at the stake for even suspicion of using PEDs.)

Finally, none of this takes into account that a steroid policy was put into effect in 2004. Apparently, the Red Sox players, including Manny Ramirez—who for years kept buying blackberries at the grocery store thinking he could use them to check his e-mail—all were smart enough to fool the tests leading up to their championships.

The argument has little merit because of its open-endedness. There are names of known users, names of nonusers, names of gnome users (those that kept gnomes in their lockers for the sake of superstition), names of those known to use known users by selling them phony stuff for a profit, and those names of unknown users known only to those that knew them.

We will never know to what extent steroids were used in baseball, but generally the time after the infamous strike of 1994 is referred to as the Steroid Era, or to Republicans as the "Clinton Ruining Another Thing Truly American Era."

So as I said before, it's a relationship straight out of the Bible. The Yankees were the younger brother of the Red Sox. The Red Sox gave them their hand-me-down clothing, which the Yankees used to win a fashion contest. Then they bragged about how cool they were.

Summary

The relationship between Martians and Uranians is biblical in nature. Instead of a bush bursting into flames, there have been instances where the teams themselves did (see the 1978 Red Sox and the 2004 Yankees).

But it would surprise most to learn how much the Red Sox contributed to the Yankees' success. These gestures are rarely referred to as the unselfish act of a rival and are almost always referred to as blatant incompetence.

Yet even with all that's transpired between the two teams, Martians are still unhappy and Uranians are still dissatisfied. Is there any way these two fan bases can look ahead and leave all the negative feelings built up in their minds behind?

Think About It

If you were Harry Frazee, what would you have done?

a. kept Babe Ruth, but benched him to teach him a lesson
b. sold the team and let the next poor sap deal with Ruth
c. hired Barbara Hershey to shoot Babe Ruth like she did Roy Hobbs
d. produced a Broadway farce based on the story of an owner ruining a baseball team

7

Avoiding an Argument

We already know what happens when we argue. Negative emotions come out and take over. No progress is made in any reasonable discussion. The popular metaphor is banging your head against a wall. Yet we continue to subject ourselves to this pattern of behavior. Albert Einstein once said, "The definition of insanity is doing something the same and expecting a different result." (I believe it was Albert; it may have been his half-brother Cornelius.)

So why do Martians and Uranians continue to fight and expect different results?

Why We Argue

These two cultures have been around for generations and have managed to coexist to some degree. Well, we haven't completely destroyed the other, that is, even though some have tried. It gets very difficult to be so restrained, and we're only human (well, Martian and Uranian). So it stands to reason that we look to guidance from above; no, not necessarily our gods (Ted Williams and Mickey Mantle, respectively), but rather the heads of our teams or role models.

Martians and Uranians began their lives together amicably because they watched as the adults played nice together, whether it was Harry Frazee of the Red Sox dealing with Jacob Ruppert or Tom Yawkey sitting down for a beer with Larry MacPhail and deciding to trade Ted Williams for Joe DiMaggio before waking up the next morning

KEY TERMS

Tom Yawkey—owner of the Red Sox for 44 seasons whose most memorable act was keeping the city's streets clean and free of parade confetti

hungover like you wouldn't believe, saying "I did *what?*" and changing his mind.

What some claim to be the first dustup came in 1938 when Red Sox pitcher Archie McKain plunked Yankees batsman Jake Powell, prompting Powell to charge the mound. That's when shortstop/manager Joe Cronin rushed in to explain to Powell with his fists that Powell should just take first base. After Powell and Cronin were ejected, they proceeded to continue their "discussion" down the runway. A similar battle arose in 1952 between loose cannons Jimmy Piersall of the Red Sox and Billy Martin of the Yankees, who went after each other off the field of play before the game even started.

Up through the 1960s, there was very little going on, save for one instance when "Gentleman" Jim Lonborg actually did a little headhunting in retaliation in 1967, but that was it. Then in 1973, everything changed when Yankees catcher Thurman Munson took off for home on what would be a missed suicide squeeze. He bowled into Red Sox catching sensation Carlton Fisk, who without missing a beat rolled on top of Munson and began pummeling him with the ball still in his hand. Well, that was all the feud needed to get humming. Red Sox pitcher Bill "Spaceman" Lee made some comments about the Yankees fighting with purses and the fuse was truly lit.

Fast-forward to 1976 when the fuse finally reached the detonator and Bill Lee found himself being dragged down by Yankees third baseman Graig Nettles. The blow ended up separating Lee's shoulder and earned him a fish in a purse courtesy of Billy Martin, who lacked no experience in fighting with Red Sox, and also apparently lacked no experience in picking out purses.

Once Martians and Uranians saw what was happening on the field, they all thought, "Whoa, we've been holding back!"

As Martians are prone to exaggerating the caliber of their players, so too are they inclined to hype the magnitude of their team's on-field scuffles as the nastiest battles ever to take place on a baseball diamond. That may be far-fetched, since Hall of Famer Juan Marichal once clubbed John Roseboro over the head with a bat. (Remind me again why Pete Rose isn't in the Hall of Fame?)

There's been no clubbing between the Red Sox and Yankees, but there's been tackling, beaning, flipping, tossing, shoulder-separating, yelling, bench-clearing, charging, arresting, protesting, booing, cheering, avenging, ejecting, fining, and suspending. And the bad blood lasts for a long time. The 1970s saw the flames ignite again before dying down until 2003 when the embers reignited. This war lasted for two years and included stuff that even the Giants-Dodgers battles never saw, for instance a couple of players being arrested for getting violent with a groundskeeper. Lest we forget former Red Sox manager and current Yankees bench coach Don Zimmer seeking out Pedro Martinez during a skirmish only to get tossed aside like yesterday's trash.

Come to think of it, if Mars and Uranus *don't* have the most heated fights in baseball history, I'd like to see who does.

Battle of Tongues

In the current-day landscape of the feud, Hank Steinbrenner, reading from the "Book of Steinbrenner," went on a rant about how Red Sox Nation is only a fabrication of the media and no one really cares about Red Sox Nation, yadda yadda yadda.

The Book of Steinbrenner

✓ Berate everyone else
✓ Make outrageous statements and stand by them
✓ Winning is the only thing
✓ Growl a lot
✓ Challenge random people to fights
✓ Market insanity
✓ Do not read the news—*make* the news
✓ Start each day by pissing someone off
✓ ABC (Always Be Crazy)
✓ Never say anything without hyperbole
✓ Stomp through a rose garden from time to time
✓ Laugh maniacally when other owners talk about increased revenue sharing
✓ Fire people who don't work for you
✓ Light cigars with money
✓ Keep a shoehorn in your pocket to throw at people
✓ Put a clause in your will that says you would like to be stuffed and mounted "in the attack position" upon your death
✓ When entering any room containing a goldfish, immediately walk to it and initiate a staring contest

John Henry, in turn, made Steinbrenner a member of Red Sox Nation. That was to show there were no hard feelings, but it was done with a smirk and a sarcastic glint in his eye. Show of good sportsmanship? Ha! Do you know how much e-mail spam comes with being a member of Red Sox Nation? One blast and Yahoo, Gmail, and AOL can all get shut down.

So that's who the subjects of each planet look toward. Monkey see, monkey do. You can't expect the fans to act differently than the most visible members of the Nation and the Empire. If an edict comes down from the top to stop wearing shirts with messages of hate on them, each side always checks to see if the front offices are wearing them underneath other shirts or backward. Then the fans do the same. Aha! Loophole.

How Arguments Hurt Us

Arguments set out to do harm to the other person, even if it's not intended that way. But the end result is that you mock, abuse, minimize, and emasculate your verbal combatant.

Mock

For being a Yankees fan or a Red Sox fan, you open yourself up to unbridled mocking. How many times have you been stereotyped just for revealing who you are? "Oh, you're a Yankees fan? I'll talk slower." "Hey, Red Sox fan, here, lemme get you a Kleenex." And so on.

Abuse

The abuse goes a step further by refusal to serve you in a store, for example. Bartenders brag about not serving customers wearing Yankees caps and cashiers immediately go on a break when someone approaches them wearing a Red Sox jersey. (I believe fanatical discrimination should be a part of our next major civil rights legislation.)

KEY TERMS

Fanatical discrimination—to make stereotypical assumptions of someone's character based on his or her allegiance to a certain team

Minimize

Your status is minimized when you're someone speaking as a Martian or a Uranian instead of just a baseball fan: "Oh, what do you know about salary restrictions? You're a Red Sox/Yankees fan."

Emasculate

As much as you don't want to believe that arguing emasculates you, it does. (Yes, even you ladies, in a figurative way, of course.) No one likes having his or her argument questioned on the grounds of insanity. No one even wants to acknowledge your notion that the Red Sox are buying umpires or that the networks are pulling for an all–New York World Series to boost their ratings.

Still Lost in Translation

I'm not here to tell you what to do in a fight (curl up in a ball on the ground until the riot police arrive). I want to teach you ways to avoid these arguments, whether they're simple verbal exchanges or something more, er, Zimmerian.

Remember how we looked at the inability to translate properly as the main reason we misunderstand each other? And how arguments stem from these misunderstandings? There are many argument circles that you can find yourself in, but a few of the most popular involve the topics of championship count, payroll, and most recently, steroids leading to invalidating the Red Sox championships. I've alluded to these arguments a lot because they come up a lot in my practice and out in the real world. It's unlikely a Martian and Uranian have spoken more than once without at least one of these topics coming up.

The key is to recognize that you are only turning the wheel in one direction and you're soon going to end up back where you started. Let's look at some popular argument-launching phrases and trace their trajectories.

"Come back to me when you have 27 championships"

Martian: "You have only been alive for seven."

Uranian: "My father was a Yankees fan and his father was a Yankees fan and his father before him was a Yankees fan."

Martian: "Fine, so your great-grandfather can brag about 27 championships then."

Uranian: "I've heard all the stories from him, so it's like I lived them."

Martian: "It took the Yankees this entire century to win again, despite the hundreds of millions they spent on free agents."

Uranian: "Yeah, well *you* haven't won since 2007."

Martian: "We've won twice in the last half-dozen years."

Uranian: "Come back to me when you have 27 championships."

"Your spending is unreasonable."

Uranian: "If you wanted to win, you could spend more."

Martian: "We can't spend that much without eventually going bankrupt."

Uranian: "You spend almost as much as we do."

Martian: "We're not even close. The difference between teams is the payroll of Seattle."

Uranian: "You're acting like you're a small-market team."

Martian: "Compared to you, we are!"

Uranian: "You have millions to spend on free agents."

Martian: "We have a budget."

Uranian: "A couple million more and you wouldn't be complaining about being outspent."

Martian: "Your spending is unreasonable."

"The Red Sox used PEDs in 2003. Therefore, their titles are tainted."

Martian: "But the Yankees won and they also had users on the team."

Uranian: "Not in the 1990s, they weren't."

Martian: "Riiiiiiiight. You think they just started taking them in the new millennium?"

Uranian: "It doesn't matter, they weren't the core of our team."

Martian: "It was Pettitte and Clemens, your two best pitchers."

Uranian: "They were not as important to the Yankees as Manny and Ortiz were to the Red Sox."

Martian: "Papi only admitted to using a supplement, not injecting himself."

Uranian: "His home runs skyrocketed from 20 to 31 in his first year out of Minnesota and then up to 54. Steroids had to have been involved."

Martian: "Babe Ruth's home-run total went from 19 to 54 in his first year in New York. Are you suggesting he did steroids, too?"

Uranian:"But the Babe was already a star. Ortiz was a bench player."

Martian: "By 2004, there was testing."

Uranian: "And you think that stopped them?"

Martian: "They passed multiple drug tests."

Uranian: "They used PEDs in 2003. Therefore, your titles are tainted."

The Devolution of Man

Clearly these arguments go in a circle. Yankees fans trumpet their successes and Red Sox fans try to cut them down. Or Yankees fans go on the attack and Red Sox fans deftly parry the blade.

Uranus point	Mars counterpoint
"You bought your championships."	"We were only buying our championships to keep you from buying them."
"Your players were on steroids."	"So were yours."
"The league wanted you to win."	"So you're saying the league was helping us when they awarded a home run to Derek Jeter after Jeffrey Maier leaned over the right-field fence?"

Each argument circle has an inciting statement, so we see how an argument might evolve and how it might *de*volve. But how do you avoid these circumstances, especially if you are in a situation that calls for civility?

Instead of looking at the reasons we need to argue, let's look at what we need to avoid arguments.

What Mars Needs to Avoid Arguments

We know that Martians argue because they want to show Uranians they're more intelligent. As we've discussed, Boston has been all about the Intelligentsia for centuries. It doesn't mean its inhabitants won't try to hurdle parking meters while intoxicated. There are several things a Martian needs in order to avoid arguments.

Equal Footing

A Yankees loss knocks Uranians down a peg and they're not in as good a position to debate. Hence, Mars is able to speak more formally and calmly, without the need to educate their rivals.

Uranians usually don't feel like arguing at that point anyway. That keeps Martians from needing to initiate defensive maneuvers, but may, however, prod them to just poke Uranians with a stick to make sure they're still alive. But they needn't go further than that.

Outbidding the Yankees

Martians know that if the Red Sox outspend the Yankees, even once, then they've lost the right to jabber on about the Yankees' reckless spending. Though one time only proves an exception to the rule, Martians do not *want* to continue debating the issue of payroll. Again, giving them equal footing assures them that Uranus won't be in an aggressive stance.

A Natural Disaster and Cataclysmic Event

It goes without saying that Martians would rather not have to resort to one of these to stop arguing, but Mars is, first and foremost, a sister planet of Uranus and remains in solidarity with it, just as long as it's about something more important than baseball. But when baseball is the most important thing at the time, Mars is content with sticking it to Uranus every chance it gets.

What Uranus Needs to Avoid Arguments

Uranians love to argue to keep Martians in their place. They love their place atop the mountain and don't wish to relinquish it. Yankees fans have their own list of things that help them avoid confrontations.

A Yankees Win

When the Yankees win, there's no need to engage Red Sox fans in any debate. Uranians, remember, are all about bottom lines and finishing what they start very quickly. They will gloat, make no mistake about that, but there's no need for them to get into semantics over who bribed which umpire to win or which player was juiced up at the time.

(At the time of the win, however, Martians will immediately ratchet up the call for a salary cap in an effort to lure Uranians back into an argument circle.)

Keeping It Civil

I try to advise my clients to not be drawn into these arguments if they do not want to be there. I tell them to be the "better man," even if they are Yankees fans. (I kid.) Here are some ways to begin a conversation safely; just remember to keep it light and tangy with a strong fruit taste, like a palette-cleansing sorbet.

Start with a Subject You Both Like (Not Baseball)

Martian: "Hey, Dave, did you catch the bass fishing extravaganza on the tube last night?"

Uranian: "Are you kidding? I couldn't turn away. I watched all six hours of it!"

Ask a Question About His Life and Act Like You Care What the Answer Is

"Dave, what's the best motor oil you've found for your car? Fascinating!"

Make an Observation That He'll Appreciate

"Did you tar that driveway yourself? Great job."

Laugh Randomly at Some Point

Not in a maniacal way, remember; you're trying to get into his good graces, and the second he thinks you're laughing *at* him or his team, you're back to square one.

Try something like, "Ha ha ha, watermelon. Oh, that's great!"

Feed Him

Do not poison the food. Remember that the way to a man's heart (and any Martian/Uranian, for that matter) is through his stomach.

Play with His Pet

If you get in good with his dog, he'll love you. If he's got a cat, the thing doesn't want you to interrupt it while it's rubbing up against you. Ignore it. If he has a fish, don't tap on the glass. If he has a boa constrictor, you probably shouldn't be over there.

Principal Rules for Avoiding an Argument

Now that the mood is set and no one is tense, the four keys to avoiding an argument altogether are not having an agenda, stop giving advice, forgoing expectations, and *being* right versus *doing* right.

Don't Have an Agenda

Starting any conversation with an agenda in mind is not a good thing. Martians may go into a conversation thinking they're going to get Uranians to admit they believe Boston fans are better than New York fans. Forget it. It's like when reporters ask a pitcher with pinpoint control if he purposefully threw at the other team's best hitter after he smacked a home run in his previous at-bat, and the pitcher says, "No, that pitch just got away from me."

Is that shocking to anyone? Did you not see that one coming? Did you put money down on the hope he'd say, "Yeah, I reared back and tossed it right at him. I was aiming for his neck, but just got him in the arm, unfortunately."

The reporter went in with the goal that he was going to get the honest answer. And reporters always look genuinely surprised when the pitcher answers the way he usually does.

The same goes for Martians trying to get Uranians to acknowledge the Yankees have been the beneficiaries of more calls during crucial situations than the Red Sox have. You're going to get stonewalled. Eliminate any thought of asking these questions, and instead ask more open-ended ones. Try something like, "What could the National League do to become more competitive with the American League?"

Stop Giving Advice

No one wants unsolicited advice, especially of the insulting variety. You definitely want to avoid any tips like:

> "No one wants to see you wearing so much eye makeup."
> "Sit up straight and maybe you won't look so dumpy."
> "Eat a salad now and again."
> "Breath mints—look into them."

Forgo Expectations

You're not going to get your counterpart to totally come around to your side. At the end of the day, Red Sox fans will be Red Sox fans and Yankees fans will be Yankees fans. It's like the Chris Rock joke about Siegfried and Roy's tiger after the tiger attacked Roy. "Everyone said that the Tiger went crazy," Rock started. "The tiger didn't go crazy, the tiger went *tiger*."

In the caverns of your head, you can hear former Arizona Cardinals football head coach Dennis Green as he screams, "They are who we thought they were!" Yankees fans resorting to violence should not surprise you either. Violence is *not* a last resort in the Bronx; it's a summer resort. They spent much of their time vacationing there.

Now there *are* some concessions you *might* hear, but you should not expect these, nor should you attempt to lead the conversation toward

Respect on Mars Means...
Paying the exorbitant $7 bag check fee at Yankee Stadium

these potentials phrases. A fan may admit to his player slumping; he may admit to his player sucking; he may admit that your pitching ace is better than his; he may admit to your ballpark being nice (Martians only); or he may say that you did deserve to win (Uranians only).

Being Right Versus Doing Right

My Martian clients are always telling me that they know they're right. And I know they're right about being right. But conveying that to your Uranian friend is another story. Do you need to go through the trouble of convincing him? Sometimes it seems that it would take that setup from *A Clockwork Orange* to sway him toward your side. Leave it be.

But doing the right thing is much easier than putting up barriers. You will at least know in your heart that you're correct, if that's any consolation...even if you're not.

Other recommendations I make for staying off argument's doorstep:

Don't raise your voice
Don't make any sudden movements toward sharp objects
Don't make condescending or sarcastic comments
Don't interrupt
Don't cross your eyes or stick your tongue out
Don't give them the "stink eye"
Don't put your sock on your hand and pretend like it's him talking

Listening Without Getting Upset

Now there is no guarantee that both parties will attempt to maintain a calm discourse. When I work with clients in my office, both are usually willing to listen and try new methods (unless the game is on in the background, in which case their emotions usually get the better of them). But you may engage with someone who is just looking for an argument. In this circumstance, you should remain calm.

Deep yoga breathing helps. One translation of the Sanskrit word *yoga* means "to unite," speaking of the mind, body, and spirit. Just as long as you don't envision your fist uniting with his face, this practice will do fine.

Politely excusing yourself and going to the bathroom works as well. If there is a window in the bathroom that leads outside, then by all means, use that. If you happen to see his car in the driveway and wish to scratch it with your keys as you walk past, then do so, but do so *calmly*.

A Caring, Gentler Rival

I know that Martians and Uranians are rugged, manly fans (even some of the women) who don't have a soft bone in their bodies, but I'm going to use the "v" word right here and I want you to know it's okay. Martians and Uranians can get *vulnerable*.

Yes, it's true. When their teams lose, they aren't in the mood to battle it out in a verbal duel of (half) wits. That's the time when you must appreciate your counterpart's state and remember what it's like to feel vulnerable.

Respect on Uranus Means...
Not screaming "THEEEEEEEE YANKEEZ WIN!" during a baptism

Sure, you can feel emboldened when your team wins, but it's only going to come back to haunt you later. It's inevitable. Sure, it might take 86 years, but it will.

Now's the perfect time to hold him in your arms and say...ha ha, just kidding, there. Boy, you should see the look on your face. In reality, don't touch him.

But seriously, how do you approach Martians and Uranians when they are upset? What do you say to them? Remember, you're trying to *avoid* an argument...at least for the sake of this chapter.

Don't say	Do say
Boy, you really choked on it	They fought hard
I loved every minute of that	Hey, it was a good series/game
You must feel awful	You're looking healthful
Wanna watch it again?	There's a Farley/Spade movie on
I am so happy right now	Think about how life is a blessing
There is a god	Look at it spiritually
What a waste of a season for you	Wanna go winter clothes shopping?

The whole lesson can be streamlined if both Martians and Uranians take something off the back end. That is, they don't need to spend as much time learning these helpful tips to making life argument-free if they just take out the major agitators from their arsenals.

Knowing what both sides need, they must leave some of that at the door, so to speak.

How Uranians Can Be Less Cruel

Stop bringing up how many championships your team has won.

When the Yankees first started winning their championships, they did so with an innovative use of their farm system, a system that most other teams did not have. Ed Barrow was ahead of the curve.

New York would develop players, then keep the best ones, naturally. It was Boston that had to outspend them. Now, the Yankees want to keep the best ones, they just have to pay a mint to do so.

But the first run of championships lasted through 1962. Since then, when other teams began to get the hang of things, they've won seven in almost 50 years. And four of those were because they were ahead of the curve after the 1994 lockout. They figured out that money would not be an issue, something it took teams like the Red Sox, the Mets, and the Cubs a while to pick up on.

The Celtics were the same way. Red Auerbach's style of play was ahead of its time. It took the league years to catch up and while they did, Red's teams were racking up the hardware. Ever since their magical run, though, the team has won six times in almost 40 years.

If a Yankees fan is in a conversation with a Celtics fan and he keeps bringing up the 17 championships his team has won, then "27" is fair game.

But talking about trophies you were not a part of is what puts Martians on the defensive.

How Mars Can Be More Accepting

And Martians must bend a little as well; if Uranians are making a concession, you mustn't provoke them. Do not bring spending into the equation. They aren't going to change the rules and if the Red Sox had the chance to spend as much as they did, you would love it.

Yes, it's frustrating that it comes down to money for most free agents, but that's the way it is in the world. Stars go where the dough is, even if the rest of us can't understand why a player would care if he made $180 million instead of $170 million. (Hey, we only play the lottery if it's over $100 million. A paltry pot of $40 million isn't going to be enough to support our lifestyle—it's really only $25 million after taxes.)

The point is, Uranians can't control the fact that they root for the team with the most revenue and seemingly bottomless pockets, even if some of them did choose the team *because* they were winning. Just let the games play out. Spending almost 50 percent more than the next highest team only promises you a spot in the playoffs (2008 excepted). After that, it's a whole new ballgame. Enjoy the show!

If you follow these tenets, you will find yourself more peaceful in the presence of rival beings. You may remain silent in their presence, but it's better than the alternative.

Arguing takes up so much time and energy. Even if you're just agreeing so you don't have to argue, that's fine. Eventually, you may begin to believe what you're agreeing with—who knows?

There's no sense in getting into an argument circle if you don't need to because you're going to go nowhere. It's like if your friend lived three miles away and you wanted to jog over to his house, but you decided to do it on your treadmill instead. You still logged three miles, but you didn't get anywhere.

Let the players and front offices follow your lead for once. If they see you shaking hands instead of plowing into one another and unloading with both fists, maybe they'll do the same. Of course, with the game on the line, when your manager gives the sign for the suicide squeeze, it may be better to do the latter.

Summary

It's easy for Martians and Uranians to get drawn into a verbal debate on any subject. Red Sox fans are always right, but Yankees fans do not agree because they are always right, too. Hence, any debate devolves into the circle of redundancy.

Instead of trying to transform the other's ideology, it is best to simply sidestep confrontation. Ignoring any bait put out by your adversary is the first step, followed by just walking away. Above all, avoid violence at all costs, no matter how difficult that may seem. Remember to B-R-E-A-T-H-E: Be Reasonably Evasive and Think Happy Emotions.

Think About It

Martians
A Uranian comes up to you and says, "Your World Series victories are tainted." What should your response be?
a. "Fine, then we'll just have our three Super Bowls."
b. "And Pettitte didn't play on your 2009 team?"
c. "You're a moron."
d. "That Jack Johnson's a mellow guy, isn't he?"

Uranians
A Martian comes up to you and says, "The Yankees just signed another big-money free agent." What should your response be?
a. "Quit your whining."
b. "As if the Red Sox couldn't afford him, too."
c. "I heard the weather's going to turn cold."
d. "It's obvious the Yankees just want to win more than the Red Sox do."

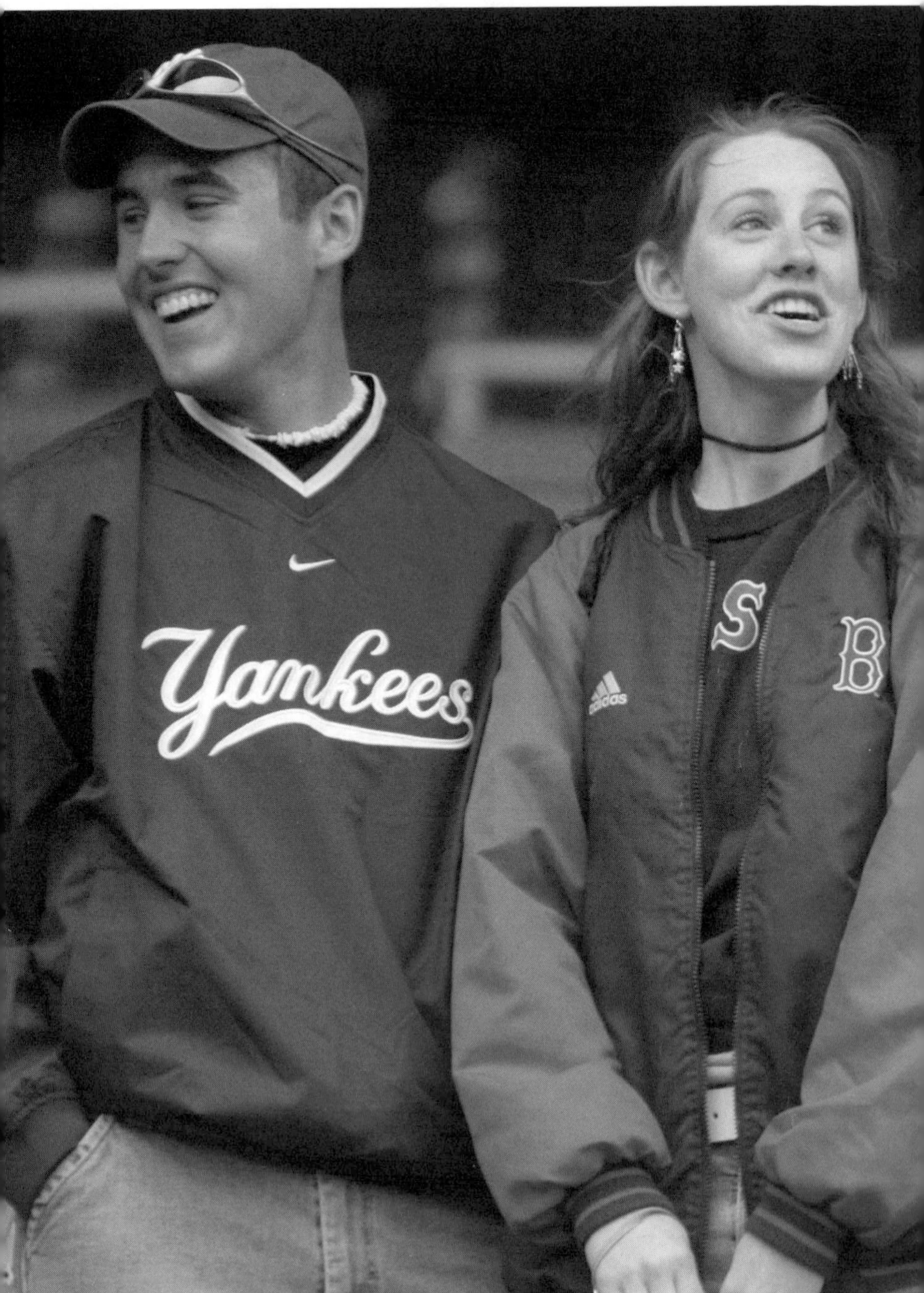
Yankees

8

Dealing with Loss

Even the greatest baseball teams in history pass away eventually. It's inevitable. The Impossible Dream Team passed on. The Big Red Machine was laid to rest. The Bash Brothers have died (and continue to die every time we see them do something stupid in public). Even with a relatively similar lineup to the previous year, these once great teams lose some of their luster. Baseball is not constructed for eternal happiness.

Grieving the Loss of a Season

Another manner in which Martians and Uranians are different is in the way they grieve. Swiss-born psychiatrist Elisabeth Kubler-Ross introduced five distinct stages in 1969 that she claimed humans go through as they suffer from a significant life event, such as losing a high-profile playoff series. It's essentially called "the death of a season." The stages include denial, anger, sadness, fear, and acceptance.

Denial

Denial is convincing yourself that something terrible hasn't really happened, or that it couldn't possibly be happening.

Uranians are big into denial because they're not used to bad things happening to them. Take 1996, for example. Derek Jeter hits an easily catchable fly ball to right field. Baltimore's Tony Tarasco settles under it only to have the ball snatched out of his hands by New Yorker Jeffrey

Maier. What should have been a routine out was called a home run, the Yankees went on to win the ALCS and subsequently the World Series, and Jeffrey Maier was interviewed on the *Late Show with David Letterman.*

That's how it works to New Yorkers. A guardian angel (in this case, a 12-year-old with a baseball mitt) always protects those, the Chosen Ones, from harm.

The A's remember watching their closer, Martian legend Dennis Eckersley, give up a game-winning home run in Game 1 of the 1988 World Series to a guy who couldn't walk. Kirk Gibson was just sitting up at home plate in a wheelchair and he *still* hit it out of the park. They were stunned at first, not wanting to believe it, and played the rest of the series in a daze. Only a year later did they finally acknowledge what had happened when they beat up on San Francisco, a city where buildings were collapsing and the people had other things on its mind. How's that for insensitive?

Fast-forward to 2004 and Alex Rodriguez is running down the first-base line. Boston's Bronson Arroyo stands in his way, his glove outstretched. A-Rod swats the ball away and aggressively takes second base. At the same time, Jeter scores to close the gap to 4–3. The umpires converge and rule that you cannot willfully knock the ball out of a fielder's glove. The home-plate umpire says, "It's illegal, and Alex, truth be told, that is kind of a jerk move." (Of course, I'm paraphrasing there. I don't think he used the word *illegal.*) The play went against New York, unlike the way things unfolded in 1996. Jeter was told to go back to second base and stay there until he had thought good and hard about what had happened. He was stunned. New Yorkers were stunned. They needed riot police to stay on the field for the rest of the game. (Steinbrenner issued an order for the police not to touch anything; otherwise it would be coming out of their paychecks.)

Ask the Doctor

Q: As a Martian, if I'm around Yankees and Mets fans, with whom should I side?

A: As I mentioned earlier, Uranians are your brothers. That said, the Mets fans..

It was the second time that game alone where the umpires had to confer on a ruling. In the fourth inning, Mark Bellhorn hit a home run into the left-field seats. It bounced off a fan, later found out to be Bob "Rubber Chest" McAfee from Westchester, and back onto the field. Yankees fans were stunned to find out that it would not be awarded to them as a single instead of a home run. Usually, anything winding up back on the field is in play, which is why they typically threw home runs hit by the opposing teams back onto the field. That, and they hadn't yet discovered eBay.

This type of mind-set is contrary to what usually happens in Boston. For example, back in 1999, Red Sox base runner Jose Offerman was called out when Chuck Knoblauch waved to him with a ball in his glove from about 10 feet away. The umpire deemed it "close enough."

Martians pelted the field with debris out of frustration but not because they didn't think something like that could happen to them. They were quite sure it could. The Yankees got all the calls. (Well, until 2004, that is.) Red Sox fans had learned a long time ago not to expect anything but the worst, and you can see how expectation and taking something for granted allows for dashed hopes.

New England Patriots fans had forgotten their humble beginnings by the end of their perfect season and strutted into the playoffs with no fear of losing. That's where you set yourself up for denial. Three championships already in the books and 18 straight wins will do that for you. I, for one, still don't remember if I watched that game or not.

Red Sox fans haven't quite reached that stage yet, thanks to a loss against the Tampa Bay Rays in the 2008 ALCS. Loss can be good, which we will discuss later. Denial stuns you for a while. Those dealing with denial hold out the wildest hopes; perhaps the commissioner will step in and rectify things or the umpires will enforce some obscure rule that states the team with the most southpaws wins automatically.

Some Uranians, as we have discussed before, are perpetually mired in denial. They are looking for any reason to chant "1918!" and to keep things as they were when the Yankees were given every advantage on top of their existing advantages.

Anger

"Someone is responsible for this and THEY...WILL...PAY!"

Yankees fans quickly turn toward anger when their team loses. The second the Yankees are dead (in the proverbial baseball sense, of course), their fans immediately lash out at anyone and everyone they can blame. It's not completely their fault—they're a product of their ownership, after all.

HE does not like to be disappointed. (HE, of course, is the Lord, thy Steinbrenner.) Neither do the fans. And anything short of an annual World Series appearance is unacceptable. They've got a right to be angry. They put in weeks, sometimes months, following this team, and for what? So they try to spend away the tears (sounds like a sappy '70s ballad, doesn't it?) with more and more free-agent signings.

Sadness

"Oh God, I promised myself I wouldn't cry."

This is usually where Martians start their grieving process. With expectations low, there is usually no anger. We can't forget Don

Zimmer was back on the bench in 1979 after orchestrating a collapse so monumental, you actually had to be trying to screw it up that badly. Even in 1986 (yes, THAT 1986), it took them a while before Bill Buckner was banished from Boston. He played another couple of years as did Bob Stanley, and John McNamara continued as the manager.

But the sadness lasted for a while. Martians scoff when Eric Idle tries to tell them to "Always Look on the Bright Side of Life." Instead of finding consolation in the fact that they were at death's door against the Angels and shouldn't have been in the World Series in the first place, they remained sad for a good 18 years more.

Red Sox fans know the phrase "Wait 'til next year" all too well.

Fear

"What if this is how it's always going to be?"

Both fan bases wallow in fear at times, but in their own special ways. Red Sox fans know how bad things can be and worry that it will be like that again. Yankees fans do worry that their best years are behind them, but they have also been through one or two resurgences, depending on how old they are. (They have gone a whopping 14 and 16 years between championships before. How did they ever manage?)

In their hearts, they know—again, given the game's current economic structure—that they probably won't have to wait long. It's a benefit to spending so much time at the anger stage. If they were more laid back, they would let titles come to them, which doesn't happen. But anger + money = better players to help them win NOW...or as soon as the right combination of those high-priced gunslingers starts playing better.

We've mentioned the other shoe, and Red Sox fans know it all too well. And if that shoe is dropped by a Yankees fan, then it's even

worse. The longer the Yankees go without winning, the more potent the torment will be when they actually do win.

Acceptance

"Ah, who cares, it's almost football season."

Red Sox fans are naturally inclined to drift into acceptance. Even in exultation—after they won Game 7 in the 2004 ALCS, propelling them past the Yankees for the first time in 100 years and into the World Series—Bill Simmons remarked how he kept "expecting them to announce a Game *8*."

It's a stance that keeps the heart from scarring any further. (Though I'm not sure it could actually scar any more than it had already.)

Good Endings Make Good Beginnings

At the end of a season, the team's manager and the front office personnel will bring the players in and have exit interviews with all of them. Now, it's not right to throw anyone under the bus publicly, at least not while the engine is still running. "We couldn't have won without him. He brought us here so we can't blame him, yadda yadda yadda," they'll say.

Do they keep that same opinion behind the scenes? Perhaps. Or they give them the ol' "vote of confidence," which in sportspeak means "We're changing the lock to his office as we speak."

The players bounce back faster than the fans. They have at least a couple million reasons (minus 10 percent for their agents) why they should. But they're told to learn from their mistakes. That's the same thing I tell my clients. How can you become a better fan during this off-season? Martians come back renewed. It's part of the process, like the regeneration of skin on a snake, but with a better analogy.

Uranians think their team must spend more money. Though as I mentioned before, from 2008 to 2009, the team spent *less* than they did the previous year, but that was only due to a down economy and the fact they had so egregiously went beyond the boundaries of reason up to that point, so there was nowhere to go *but* down.

Heal This!

Acceptance is the first step toward feeling better. It's one of four healing emotions that you should get familiar with. We learned of all the emotions we feel, but haven't talked about channeling each emotion and using it instead of letting it use us.

Once we learn how to control these emotions, we will see how they can help us to get through our hardships.

After acceptance, we have:

Optimism

"There's always next year" is the most optimistic phrase there is (right after "The Red Sox have outbid the Yankees on the All-Star free agent in the prime of his career"). The opposite is "Oh God! There's no tomorrow. We're doomed! We're all doomed!"

Love

Sure, it sounds a little flower power, daddy-o, but give it a shot. Try repeating the phrase "Oh, I just think it's great that the Phillies won the World Series. They earned it." Or "I love that you gave us great competition this year." If you can keep your lunch down long enough to say it, you may find yourself a little more at peace.

For a time, I would give "appreciation rocks" to all Martians and Uranians that came into my office looking for help in mourning their losses. The rocks were meant to remind them of all the things they should appreciate in their sports worlds. Unfortunately, they just threw them at each other. So I stopped giving them away.

Surprise

Surprise is a healing emotion. Are you surprised to learn that? Okay, forget I said anything. Y'know, surprise is a healing emotion. *Now* are you surprised?

Testimonial

Thanks to Dr. Wasif, I find myself much more connected to my brethren from up I-95. I still hate them, but at least now I know why.

—Sam, da Bronx

Allow yourself to be surprised sometimes. When you expect something to happen and it doesn't, you're disappointed. But if you don't expect it to happen and it does, that's surprise.

Uranians tend to set the bar too high, as I mentioned earlier. That can precipitate denial. When you're going for that high jump and the bar is so high that you actually clear the bar by jumping *under* it, without so much as touching it, then that's setting the bar a little too high.

Hope for the best, expect the worst, I recommend to all my clients, even the Uranians. And then, just accept it. Make your mantra "It is what it is."

Why do people answer the phone to tell you they're too busy to talk and will call you back instead of just letting it go to voicemail? It is what it is.

Why do you get charged more money when you overdraw your bank account because you have no more money? It is what it is.

Why are sportswriters reluctant to vote for designated hitters as Most Valuable Players, yet they will select pitchers who play once every five games? Say it with me now: It is what it is.

Coping with Stress on Mars

We all have our own individual ways to deal with stress. Short of running over your Martian or Uranian neighbor with a car, here are some ways my clients unwind:

Turning to football season
Burning team clothing
Denying anything ever happened
Drinking herbal tea
Putting on scuba equipment and sitting at the bottom of the pool
Listening to old Mel Allen broadcasts
Listening to a Yanni record
Smashing Yanni records with a hammer
Putting a whole package of Pop Rocks in your mouth and drinking a soda
Firing an employee without cause

There's something Dr. John Gray talks about in his relationship guide books you may have heard of. He likes to use what he calls the 90-10 principle. Ninety percent of what we're angry or depressed about happened in the past; only 10 percent of the stuff we focus on at this moment, what we think we're upset with, is actually related to current events.

Most of what Red Sox fans react to happened in the past. If it's a home run to win the game like A-Rod hit against them in August of '09, it brings back memories of Aaron Boone or Bucky Dent. A-Rod himself had never been a threat and wasn't a player Boston loathed. On the contrary, he'd provided them with some great fodder over the years.

When a Red Sox fan panics during a three-game losing streak, it's not the streak itself, but the experience living in their heads. For they've seen three-game losing streaks derail a season in the past, and that's what they're reacting to.

In recent memory, they've witnessed firsthand that three-game losing streaks are nothing to worry about. They know that the season is long and even a three-game losing streak to the Yankees in October is not insurmountable. When they react to it, they're reacting to what a three-game losing streak *used to* represent.

It's much easier to cope these days because there's more confidence. Sure, there has always been hope, but it was of the "I hope that hoping is going to work" variety. But now that they've seen hope work, twice, they can truly believe it will happen again.

(Red Sox fans have been beaten down so much, there is an inherent lagging indicator to their confidence.)

Martians mainly cope through artistic expression. Posting rants online, calling talk radio, and uploading humorous videos to YouTube all provide Red Sox fans with outlets for their angst. It provides them an alternative to violence. Red Sox fans write about every angle there is, every important season, each remarkable player, and the cast of characters associated with the team.

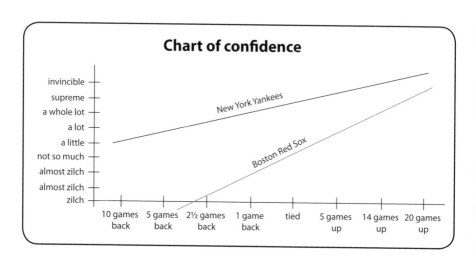

Chart of confidence

You can find videos that are both self-deprecating and pieces of social commentary, mainly on Boston's status as the once downtrodden and now most interesting team in the country, but also about its rivalry with the Yankees.

A favorite of mine is the ESPN promo where Jorge Posada and Big Papi are seated across the table from one another in a conference room, when the Red Sox DH remarks on the unworn look of Posada's hat. "I'm a catcher," says Posada. "I don't wear a hat."

With that, Papi takes the hat from him to demonstrate how to break it in. He bends it a couple of times, then puts it on his head to shape it. At that moment, Wally the Green Monster walks by the conference room and sees Papi wearing a Yankees cap. He's stunned and saddened, leaving Papi to plead that he has a good explanation for this transgression.

It's classic social commentary. As is the scene in *Ocean's Twelve* where the 12 thieves wish to stage a fight on a train in order to create a diversion. One takes a seat across from another with a table in between them and places his Red Sox cap on the table. The other immediately slams his Yankees cap on the table and IT IS ON!

Or the old local spot on Mars where a bald Johnny Damon sits in the clubhouse, brushing his luxurious, flowing wig before indulging in a cool beverage from Dunkin' Donuts, when Theo Epstein walks in on him. Johnny asks him not to tell anyone that he's actually bald. Theo agrees to do it on the condition that Johnny keeps getting him Coolattas from Dunkin' Donuts.

Respect on Mars Means...
Not urinating on property with Yankees paraphernalia featured prominently

Respect on Uranus Means...
Never mentioning any word with "Buck" as the root

This is how Martians deal with pain. It's also how they deal with joy. Through any media, any outlet, and any avenue necessary, they will send their thoughts out to the world.

Living in the Present

Live for the moment, I always say. Of course, sometimes that moment is made miserable for you by another team with a better group of starters and a deeper bullpen. In that case, find a reason to enjoy the next moment, which will be coming soon enough.

If you can't be holding a sign at a parade about how your boss thinks you have the flu, then find another activity in which you can find happiness. Use the time to come up with great new signs for next year. Try anagrams. They're super fun! Here's one for you:

> Every
> Sports fan likes when you
> Program Red Sox
> Nation on your schedule

Ah, well, you have the whole off-season to come up with something better.

Reliving the Past

Living in the past is not good. Uranians are more likely to do this as they've had a happier past. Martians would rather not think about what happened long ago. It's like having to celebrate Father's Day when every memory you have of him was kicking your toy poodle. (Even Michael Vick wouldn't kick a toy poodle, would he?)

But reliving the past to understand how you got to where you are is important. It's part of who you are, your history. Uranians may not know that the farm system their team developed was one of the first and the best. That's how they won so many championships, by being ahead of the curve.

Then, after the strike in 1994, they were one of the first to realize they could spend like crazy people with no repercussions except for a little luxury tax and, hey, they were already spending anyway, so what's an extra few dozen million dollars?

Triggering Repressed Memories

You have to be careful about reliving the past, though, since intertwined among some good memories have been some repressed ones, tucked away for years, sometimes decades, deep in the recesses of the mind.

For example, Wendy was married to Ted, who was a huge Red Sox fan. Wendy, on the other hand, didn't know much about sports. She came into my office, very frightened of Ted's reaction when she told him she had a little dent in her car. I told her not to worry; Ted didn't think the dent was a problem. But the word brought up such bad memories that he had an emotional release. (Remember that *Bucky* is a trigger word from Chapter 5.)

Coping with Stress on Uranus

Uranians have always experienced winning. Though a small part of their brain contains fear, they cope by picking up another sport and ignoring baseball. They don't want to watch the World Series if they're not in it. The year doesn't count. Wipe it clean.

Testimonial

I grew up eating, sleeping, and breathing baseball. But the more the war between the Yankees and Red Sox escalated, the more unhappy I became. Eventually, I snapped. Dr. Wasif helped me to rebuild my reputation and learn to love the game again.

—D. Zimmer, Tampa, FL

New Yorkers have many options once baseball season is over to hold their attention. It's the city that never sleeps. And also, it's the city that doesn't remind you 24/7 what's going on with their team like a certain Martian planet does.

In the case of Uranus, the 90-10 Principle is different; 90 percent of their problems have been crammed into 10 percent of the time. Yankees fans have only had to deal with strife for most of this current decade. As Steinbrenner once pointed out, the 1980s were the first decade without a Yankees win after they began their amazing run. During that time, Boston remained unfulfilled as well, so there was no antagonist. With the tables turned, Yankees fans found themselves seeking solace, which was a unique experience to them.

Becoming Whole Again

Recovery is not easy after having your heart broken. It is a restorative process that takes months, sometimes even years. Each loss takes a piece of your soul. After 1986, Boston fans bounced back quickly, but that was due to a repression of what had happened.

The initial shock was stunning, but the next spring, they met the season with optimism. They had the same great players and the same great ace, Roger Clemens. But when 1988 came and 1990 came and

Ask the Doctor

Q: How many days should I ignore Uranians after the Yankees win a world championship?

A: I never subscribe to ignoring a problem. That's like sweeping it under the carpet. But if you could take a vacation for, say, 12 months, that couldn't hurt.

Boston, specifically Roger Clemens, couldn't advance to the World Series, fans became increasingly more despondent. It became harder to bounce back.

The 2003 season left the same feeling, while 1995 and 1999 were similarly demoralizing, yet not as stunning. There was hope, but the team didn't really sell it. Stranger things had happened, but that was with more magical teams. Any advancement really would have been a miracle. In 2003 they were expecting greatness.

Yankees fans take things harder. When the *Titanic* went down, there were a lot of people who were too shocked to move. That is because they were crammed onto life boats cursing their travel agents.

The Yankees were the *Titanic*—they'd won four out of five championships, and earned a trip to the World Series six out of eight years. Then came 2004. Lives were lost that night. The S.S. *Steinbrenner* couldn't get there in time to pick up the few survivors. Despite the Yankees' championship in 2009, the team hasn't been the same since 2004 and the fans have been jarred from their perch of dominance.

Red Sox fans have really never been whole, so it's easy for them to regroup after devastating losses. They're missing a part here, a part there. They're like the zombie in those zombie movies: you shoot them in the heart and they just keep coming. There might be a hole in their chest or their arm might be cut off, but they can still push forward.

As we've discussed, part of the Uranian upbringing, part of their very being, was the ability to yell "1918!" That's been taken away from them. Nothing they say, nothing they do now can bring that back to them. The cruise had started off so well until they had decided to get too close to the Idiotberg inhabited by a bunch of fun-lovin', karaoke-singin', Jack Daniels–swiggin' wild and crazy guys. Then they got burned.

When one planet is in its mourning phase, the other may seek an opening and attempt to agitate their counterpart.

How Martians React When Uranians Need to Gloat

Red Sox fans become very defensive. They can start a "Yankees Suck" chant in a matter of seconds. It's really quite impressive. It doesn't matter where they are. It could be the symphony, a Patriots parade, a Greek Orthodox wedding—whatever the occasion, insert a minimum of two Red Sox fans, sprinkle with a little bit of spunk, and you've got a chant a-brewing.

It's been used during celebrations, but mainly, it provides a mindless buffer against Yankees fans' insults.

How Uranians React When Martians Seek Revenge

Yankees fans become aggressive. Typically, Red Sox fans drive Yankees fans nuts. When they're not whining, they are winning. And when they are winning, they become more overconfident and look to pay back Yankees fans for the shabby treatment they received for decades (remember the 90-10 Principle).

Drinking in a good victory gives them the elixir they need to be able to tell the Yankees fans off. But the Uranians do not wish to give up their status of lording over Red Sox fans, so they have to continue to puff out their chests further than Red Sox fans.

Take the incident in New Hampshire in the summer of 2007. Some Red Sox fans were crowing to a drunken Yankees fan. The Yankees fan, sensing her position was being threatened, could only elevate the game by running over one of the Red Sox fans.

Now, when I say she "could only elevate the game by running over one of the Red Sox fans," I mean that she had many options such as saying nothing or calling a cab to get her home. Or maybe calling the Red Sox fans names until one of them cried. Yep, a good ol' fashioned insult fest.

I recommend to all my clients that they use visualization in this case and this usually works. Instead of being aggressive, I ask that they visualize aggressive behavior, then smile. I believe a "happy place" for some fans is in a violent world…and that's okay. Just don't actually follow through on it, especially with a car. Use a unicycle or pogo stick or a superball to try to hurt them. Anything more is uncalled for.

Throughout a season, Martians and Uranians find different topics on which to clash. But the fact is none hit harder than the inevitable demise of a season. By the end of the year, at least one of them will find themselves in a more precarious position than the other, stung by the cold hard truth that is playoff elimination.

Each fan base has its own techniques and processes to weather the emotional storm, and to prepare itself for the rebirth that always comes the next year.

After all, every good thing must come to an end, even curses…unless there's a billy goat involved. Those things are stubborn little buggers.

Summary

Your team will lose eventually. It's one of the facts of life. (The others are Blair, Tootie, Jo, and Natalie.) How each fan deals with it is part of what differentiates Martians from Uranians.

To Martians, the scar tissue from many, many painful cuts protects them somewhat from future stings. Loss is more the norm than the exception. In a sense, they are better suited for this annual rite of passage. What doesn't kill them makes them stronger, and also allows them to drink more.

Uranians treat loss as a stunning affront to all mankind. They are less equipped to properly navigate the mourning period as outlined by Elisabeth Kubler-Ross, preferring to blow right past the 1–10 emotional scale and just start at 11.

Think About It

Imagine a doomsday scenario and then practice running through the five stages of loss from denial to anger to sadness to fear to acceptance. The better you become at it, the easier it gets. Make a game of it. Use a different accent while acting out each stage.

9

Finding Common Ground

It's not easy for Martians to forge a relationship with Uranians or for Uranians to spend time with Martians. As they say, "Relationships are like investing…with Bernie Madoff. More than likely, you're going to get burned, and in the end, somebody pays."

If you come into my office located in Kenmore Square looking for counseling, I'm going to put you to work. Oh, not vacuuming the rugs or anything like that (although the bookshelf gets pretty dusty). I put my clients through many exercises to increase understanding about where the other is coming from. It's all with the hope that someday, we can take two distant creatures and bring them to meet on middle ground, at least for an afternoon.

One tale I like to tell is an interesting story from 1943, when World War II was taking young men eligible for the draft and sending them overseas to fight for their country. About 600 of these young men played professional football. And there was a good contingent who played either for the Pittsburgh Steelers or the Philadelphia Eagles. Separately, the two teams could no longer field a regulation football squad.

President Roosevelt had made a plea for organized sports to go on during the war, as the public needed their entertainment. So, to accommodate the request, the Steelers and the Eagles joined forces to make one team—the Steagles!

Steelers owner Art Rooney only had six men under contract while Philly had 16. But the league needed at least eight teams to keep from folding, so he had to act fast.

They played one season together and then the Eagles could, once again, field their own team. But by putting their differences aside, they managed a 5–4–1 record, showing how a little compromise between owners who put their differences aside could make history. The league went on.

I ask any Martian or Uranian that comes to me seeking guidance to envision a day when we may need to get creative to keep baseball in this country going. Imagine if Boston's entry into the league had to merge with the New York entry to become…are you ready for this? The Bronxton Yank Sox! No? Okay, how about the Fen York Redkees?

Well, the name's not really important. Just imagine our country was in a pickle and President Alec Baldwin (or President Chuck Norris, if you prefer) asked us to keep baseball going while the country gets through its toughest hour. And imagine that Hank Steinbrenner's son, Little Hank, and Larry Lucchino had decided to merge their two teams, putting the needs of their country before their teams'.

KEY TERMS

Allan Huber "Bud" Selig—the current commissioner of baseball, he has overseen many key moments in recent baseball history including the 1994 strike, introduction of the wild card and interleague play, moronic scheduling, raising the stakes at the All-Star Game, revenue sharing, the World Baseball Classic, and the spread of steroids. He plans to retire when his contract expires in 2012, giving him a few more years to screw up other stuff

What would it be like? Your rival, whom you have always had nothing but contempt for, is now high-fiving you as their shortstop throws it to our second baseman who tosses it over to their first baseman for a tailor-made Yank Sox 6-4-3 double play. And we'd go on to beat the newly formed Los Angeles of Anaheim Dodgels in a seven-game series for the crown. You can get a taste of it when you watch the All-Star Game and Jeter, Pedroia, and Youkilis turn it, but we all know that isn't real, contrary to what Bud Selig tries to tell us.

Now, how would you feel if the world was turned upside down, if right was left, if day was night, if Donald Trump was mute? Would you act any differently if you knew it was going to only be one season or if it was going to be forever?

Many, though not all, of my Uranian clients say that if they knew it was for only one season, they'd just forget about baseball and wait for football season when they could enjoy their Newffalo Giant Bills.

Martians are more willing to make it work. They see a burden lifted off their backs. They see the promise of trips to each other's cities where one can wear his hat proudly without getting hazed. They see a perpetual contender for the World Series. But most of all, they see themselves going around bragging about those 27 + 7 championships their franchise has. Oh, that idea feels good to Martians.

So picture that world when talking to the other side. It doesn't have to be so cantankerous. You're not forced to hate the other. It's a free country. (Actually, it *was* a free country until President Norris took office and knocked out the Bill of Rights with a roundhouse kick.)

One side note to that hypothetical thought experiment is that a team called the Boston Yanks actually *did* exist. They were a football squad for four years before eventually leaving Boston due to lack of interest. They spent time as the New York Bulldogs, then the New York Yanks, and finally ended up in Dallas. After that, if you follow the trail

> ## Testimonial
>
> Being from New York but living in Boston, I'm grateful for Dr. Wasif's help in dealing with the whiny, bed-wetting, ignorant Martians I have to work with. It's not easy being a kindergarten teacher.
>
> —Kathy K., Somerville, MA

a little further, you'll see that they maintain a small link to what became the Baltimore Colts. See, we're not as far apart as you think.

Boston and New York together could be magical. They could be baseball's version of a rock supergroup, maybe like The Traveling Wilburys only with not as many guitarists.

Man in the Mirror

We've covered the differences between Martians and Uranians, but what about their similarities? These are areas where they can relate. As we learned in Chapter 7, in an effort to avoid an argument, it is often enough to take a deep breath and connect to your rival through something other than the Yankees and Red Sox.

Many people don't know that *West Side Story* was the tale of feuding Martians and Uranians. Of course, the Sharks were the Yankees fans and the Jets were the Red Sox fans. (Are you kidding? A bunch of Irish street thugs? Did you not pick up on that before now?) And after a little strife, that ended fantastically well. So there is hope…

Wait, I think I'm getting that mixed up with *The King and I*. Come to think of it, the body count was pretty high in *West Side Story*. Never mind. Forget I said anything. (Note: You're wondering why a baseball book would have half a dozen references to musicals, and not one of them is *Damn Yankees*. I know. Odd, isn't it?)

But the similarities between Martians and Uranians are abundant. Think about them. It's like that scene in the Marx Brothers movie *Duck Soup* where Harpo pretends to be the mirror reflection of Groucho. They look similar, too similar to notice anything right off, but one of them is a few inches shorter than the other, has curly blond hair, and carries a horn.

Look at how many things both sides already have in common:

- They both hate Angels fans.
- They think people from the other city are worse drivers.
- They don't understand what it's like to go half a mile without seeing a Dunkin' Donuts.
- They have no problem wearing shorts outside as long as it's over 20 degrees.
- They cross the street whenever they want.
- They know how to ride the subway.
- They hate each other's accents.
- They think the Tampa Bay Rays are a nuisance.

One way we can begin to cultivate our commonalities is to look at all the similar things we find funny. It's good to have a sense of humor, to not take ourselves so seriously. Take a recent story in *The Onion* that reported on the "Jason Varitek shift" employed by Minnesota manager Ron Gardenhire, in which outfielders take a knee and the infielders move up. Of course, if there are runners on base, then Gardenhire just has the outfielders come up and play the bases. Amusing.

Now whether or not this was written by a Yankees fan or by a self-deprecating Red Sox fan remains to be seen, but if you saw Jason Varitek hit during his last couple of years in Boston, you'd realize it's pretty funny. A nice little icebreaker to lighten the tone. But obviously, if you're from Uranus, you should take as much as you give; otherwise it might lose its humor on a Martian. So in the interest of fairness, remember when Frank Costanza, George's dad on *Seinfeld*, yelled at George Steinbrenner about his poor player personnel decisions? Yes, Mr. Steinbrenner's an easy target, so you can keep lobbing softballs in his direction.

Martians and Uranians understand the gag in each of these bits. It puts us into the same frame of mind, and that's the whole concept of finding common ground: being inside the other's head and understanding why things aren't working out. Otherwise, it's like trying to hammer that round peg into the square hole.

How about a true-life anecdote that both planets can appreciate? During the 1990s, my college roommates and I had what was called an "answering machine." (Some of you kids reading this book will have to ask your parents what it was, but the best explanation is it was like voicemail, but it took up space on your end table.)

Well, one roommate was accepted for an internship with WPIX in New York City. Former Yankees great and spokesman for The Money Store Phil Rizzuto himself called the dorm to ask him about being a part of his radio show.

Our answering machine kicked on and told the Scooter, "Hi, you've reached Watson Room 328. None of us can come to the phone right now, so if you can leave a message, the person you're calling will get back to you as soon as he wants."

"Hello, Ray, this is Phil Rizzuto calling to confirm you interning for my show," Scooter said.

Well, my roommates thought it would be funny to use Phil's incoming message as the *outgoing* message on our machine. About a week later, Phil calls back only to hear his own voice saying, "Hello, Ray, this is Phil Rizzuto calling to confirm you interning for my show."

Phil's second message began with a long pause: "Uh, hello? Listen, I'm not sure if I've got the right number, but I'm calling for Ray. This is Phil Rizzuto…" The Scooter was never the same after that, but it sure busted up a bunch of college kids, from both the Uranian and Martian side of the tracks.

See, common ground is the ground upon which you can both laugh (even if it comes at the expense of a baseball legend).

R-E-S-P-E-C-T

Throughout this book, we've learned the emotions that come to the surface, the misunderstandings we experience, and the disputes we engage in all stem from a lack of communication. (Well, that and a deep dislike of the other side.)

Most of us jump right into arguments without asking ourselves questions like "Where is he coming from?" "What is he trying to say?" and "How many licks does it take to get to the Tootsie Roll center of a Tootsie Pop?"

I find a helpful exercise to do is what I like to call the "Respect Letter." It is a way to put your feelings down on paper and allow the other side to read it, instead of talking over one another. The idea of the letter is to say, "Here's what's on my mind…," but to do it in a way that is direct yet kind, firm yet understanding. And you can do it without negative impulses getting in the way, taking over and driving your thoughts toward the dark side. You can say exactly what you want to say and how you want to say it. Then you'll get a fair chance to be heard and, equally, to hear a rebuttal.

Sometimes it feels like Martians and Uranians are having one-sided conversations with each other. Martians want Uranians to understand that the job Joe Torre did with the Yankees was overrated, but the

Uranians aren't listening. They're too busy trying to tell Martians that their ballpark is old and decrepit and smells like wet sausages.

In a respect letter, you construct each short paragraph around the following emotions: anger, sadness, fear, regret, and respect. After explaining how his actions make you angry, sad, fearful, and regretful, you finish on a positive note by explaining what it is you respect about him. This way, he can leave feeling you really do care about the relationship and that it's important to make strides to relieve your frustrations.

After you sign it (you're free to use a smiley face or little heart if you'd like), you construct a short paragraph as a postscript that tells him what you'd want to hear in his response letter to you.

I used to tell my clients to deliver it to their counterpart in person after our session, but they all ended up taping it to a rock and throwing it through the window. It's been a learning experience for me, as I have come to the conclusion that I can't allow Martians and Uranians the opportunity to throw things under any circumstances.

Here are some stories about Martians and Uranians trying to get along, and the letters they've written under my advisement (I've kept the names the same, but changed some of the verbs so as to maintain their anonymity).

A Respect Letter About Fairness

Mary and Randall have been married for just over three years now and though their parents disowned them both upon learning that it would be an interfanatical marriage, the two were steadfast in their love for one another. One evening, the Red Sox played the Yankees in a game the Yankees won in extra innings, when Jeter was awarded a ground-rule triple with two outs and a man on first on a ball that bounced into the stands in right-center field. Terry Francona argued, but to no avail.

This came after a Kevin Youkilis grand slam was negated when Youk was called out for using too much pine tar on his goatee, a seldom-enforced rule.

The couple had a big quarrel about that, and was leaning toward a trial separation when they agreed to meet with me. I told them to think greatly about what they were feeling and how it affected their love for one another before putting it onto paper. Here is what Mary wrote:

Dear Randall,

Angry...I am so mad right now, I can spit. The Yankees won again due to two horrendous calls. How could the umpires hand the game to the Yankees like this?

Sadness...It is very sad to think that the umpires would have such low moral fiber that they would stoop to taking bribes from the Yankees organization and for the soulless people involved to dare pay them off to begin with.

Fear...I fear the world has gone to hell in a handbasket and that you are driving the bus.

Regret...I regret not listening to my parents. I regret the fact that they've moved and I no longer know how to get a hold of them.

Respect...I respect that you don't clip your toenails in the bedroom anymore.

Yours truly,

Mary

P.S. I would like you to respond that the umpires made a terrible call and are obviously being paid off by the Yankees, and that you will not be renewing your season tickets until some Yankees officers are prosecuted to the fullest extent of the law.

Here is Randall's letter:

> Dear Mary,
> I am leaving you. I have found a way cooler girl. Not only is she studying to be a cosmologist or cosmetologist or something like that, but she's a Yankees fan. Good luck living with that crappy team of yours.
> Respectfully yours,
> Randall
> P.S. Jeter could've had three bases if he wanted. That's why they gave him a triple.

After our successful session, Mary and Randall jointly decided to drop the "trial" from their separation.

A Respect Letter About Karma

For years, cousins Jared and Nick would get together on Arbor Day as their families had for years when they were children. There never seemed to be a problem when the Yankees were winning and the Red Sox were losing. Nick would strut around with a creaseless Yankees cap on his head chanting "1918!" while Jared would just keep his head down and say nothing, though he secretly hated Nick's behavior.

As is the case with so many clients I've worked with, the levee broke in 2003. Jared didn't think he'd be able to take another Arbor Day with his cousin. Then the Red Sox won in 2004 and Arbor Day was never the same again. Jared had built up such hostility that it all came out. Nick played the victim and tried to grasp where it was coming from.

Dear Jared,

Angry…I am angry to see you treating me with such contempt when I've never done anything to deserve this.

Sadness…I am so sad to think that we are related and that seems to mean nothing to you.

Fear…I'm afraid that I'll never be able to look at you the same way again.

Regret…I regret that I spent so many weeks and months consoling you when your team lost. And now this is how you treat me?

Respect…I respect how we could always sit down and have a root beer when the Yankees won.

Your cousin,

Nick

P.S. I would hope that you apologize to me for making me feel inferior and like a second-class citizen. I'm not even that big a baseball fan; I really only follow the Knicks. You should know that.

I encouraged Jared to respond immediately, and here is what he wrote:

Dear Nick,

I'm sorry, I couldn't understand you. I think you have something stuck in your throat. HAHAHAHAHAHAHAHA HAHA!!!!!! CHOKE!!!

Your cousin,

Jared

I actually think that one went pretty well.

A Respect Letter About Validity

Yankees fan Newie was upset when he heard the news about Big Papi testing positive for a banned substance and even more upset that his friend JD was nonplussed about the whole thing.

Yo JD,

Angry...I am beside myself with anger when I think about the fact that I wasted five years of my life not being able to chant "1918!" when it turns out I could've been doing it the whole time.

Sadness...It's sad to think that the only way your team can win is to cheat.

Fear...I'm afraid you're exactly what I've always thought you were, and that is a whiney little pathetic loser, just like your team.

Regret...I regret that I sold my 2004 Yankees World Series shirt on eBay that I had made when we were up 3–0. It looks like they're going to have to replay that series after all, with the Yankees against the Cardinals in the World Series.

Respect...I've always respected how you can get your hair to stay perfectly straight even when we're going down a roller coaster.

Newie

P.S. I hope you will join me in my letter-writing campaign to the Boston Red Sox front office to convince them the only right thing to do is to return their trophies.

Again, I encouraged a response from JD:

> Dear Newie,
>
> I have, indeed, started a letter-writing campaign. My first letter was to the State Board of Psychiatrics. They would like to meet you. I made an appointment for next Tuesday. Please clear your schedule.
>
> JD

A Respect Letter About Elimination

Bill and Phil work together in the accounting department at an insurance company. Their desks face each other in the bullpen area. In 2009, Bill knew he was going to hear it from Phil because the Yankees had advanced in the playoffs and the Red Sox had not.

> Dear Phil,
>
> Angry…I am angry that the Yankees have bought their way into another World Series championship. I mean, what is it going to take for the other owners in the league or the commissioner or someone to put a stop to such an atrocity?
>
> Sadness…It saddens me to think that I'm not going to be able to experience the sanctity of the game with my son as my father did with me because it's turned into such a mockery of what the game used to be.
>
> Fear…I am afraid that you are going to start gloating as if *you've* done something good with your life. I mean, it's unreasonable for you to be proud of anything. You're 35 years old, you've had this job for a decade with no hope of advancement, and you still live with your parents. Have you even kissed a girl? I've never heard you mention one in all the time I've been here.

Regret…I regret the fact that I used up all of my sick days getting over the stomach bug I got on that cruise to Bermuda so I will be stuck sitting next to you while you watch highlights of A-Rod's home run on YouTube.

Respect…I respect the fact that you use your headphones when listening to the game at your desk while dodging your work duties.

Respectfully yours,

Bill

P.S. I would like you to finally get your head out of your butt and realize that rooting for a team that's so far in the bag with the league is a waste of time. I also would like you to respond by agreeing with me.

Phil's response did little to ease the tension in their office.

Dear Bill,

Suck on it!

With respect,

Phil

P.S. Don't bother me today; I'm busy moving all of Kate Hudson's movies up in my Netflix queue.

Unfortunately, Phil spray-painted his response on Bill's desk, which is not how I would recommend it be done.

Lightning Round Letters

Sometimes when pairs come into my office and we don't have a lot of time, I challenge them to write down the first thing that pops into their heads with the other person sitting right in front of them. A typical example:

Angry...You suck!

Sadness...I am sad that you suck!

Fear...I'm afraid you will continue to suck!

Regret...I regret that you don't even know you suck.

Respect...I respect that you make me look less sucky.

P.S. What I would like to hear from you is "I know you're right and I'm going to make it all better by throwing myself out of a window."

But even in this example, at least you have the opportunity to get something off your chest. You're clarifying your feelings *without* yelling and interrupting. That's the main goal. These people are not hurling rocks at each other (anymore) or running each other over with their cars. Moving the negative energy from your heart to a piece of paper is a very powerful way to communicate. It's important to see that the other feels exactly the same way you do.

The best times to write these letters, when you need them most, are after a game, before an important game, during the playoffs, as spring training is beginning, when the teams are tied in the standings, when your team is behind in the standings, during the annual owners meetings, during the annual general managers meetings, during *American Idol*, when stuck in traffic, when on the subway, when in the sauna, during pregame festivities...anytime is a good time, really.

Finally, if you have anger management issues, you probably should not be equipped with sharp objects. I would suggest writing with a crayon or using finger paints to get your thoughts across.

Back Away from the Cliff

In the middle of 2009, I treated two Uranians in my office named Dante and Spero. (Sounds like a bad vaudeville joke: "These two Uranians walk into an office…" but bear with me.) It seems the two of them were having a disagreement over whether or not the Yankees bought championships. These were not Martians, by the way, but Uranians. I was impressed that one of them was adopting a deeply unpopular Martian belief.

As I mentioned in Chapter 5, saying "the Yankees buy championships" is a misleading statement. What Martians mean when they say that is, "The Yankees *attempt* to buy their championships."

I allowed Dante to speak first since he was the more agitated.

Now that the Yankees are back in their rightful place and tracking toward another successful season, the trolls are out in full force talking about "buying championships." Well, they're wrong, and I have the stats to prove it.

The Yanks do not *buy* championships; they reward homegrown players. A rough calculation that takes the percentage of salaries awarded to homegrown players versus free agents supports this claim: 39 percent of the Yankees' payroll is spent on homegrown players. The Red Sox allocated only 15 percent of their salary on homegrown players.

So which team is "buying" and "building" via free agency? It's obvious to me the Yankees are building.

Spero's shoulders slumped and I noticed he had grown tired of hearing the same argument from his friend. "Spero," I said, "why don't you explain your position to Dante?"

Wow. I am just flabbergasted. I mean, I'm a Yankees fan but you can't deny we try to buy championships. You want to talk percentages? The Yankees have spent 40 percent more than the Red Sox. There is a difference of $80 million between the two, which could pay for the Marlins' roster almost three times over. My whole thing about trying to buy a ring? Who the heck cares? It is like saying that guy drives faster because he can afford a nicer car. If you have it, you have it.

"Now, Dante, do you understand what Spero is trying to tell you?" I asked. But Dante wasn't listening. He countered his fellow fan's claim with this strained analogy: should *The Godfather* be criticized just because it had an all-star cast?

Dante was rationalizing his position and manipulating the facts. My job was to bring Dante to the common ground on which his friend was standing. In my professional opinion, Dante was on the Cliffs of Craziness. Any further and he would've fallen into Insanity Gulch. I wanted to pull him away from the edge and over to safe territory.

(By the way, *The Godfather* didn't have an all-star cast when the movie was made. Time proved that the actors were top-notch, but they weren't household names at the time of casting. It looks like they had great scouting personnel on that film. Had the studio that produced it not been able to spend money re-signing the principal talent once that talent started getting accolades, they would have had to look elsewhere to fill the roles. Charles Grodin may have been the only actor available for what they could afford to pay. Could you imagine him as Michael Corleone? Maybe Peter Falk as a young Vito Corleone. I think the analogy to *The Godfather* is best used on a team like the Twins or the Brewers, teams that continuously develop high-quality players who go on to become so much more on other teams. But I digress.)

The point is, Spero was right. It is what it is. The Yankees do buy a greater part of their contending teams than not. But that's how the game works nowadays. If they didn't, at one point over the past 20 years they would've had to say, "Well, golly, Jeter and Mariano are both coming up for extensions this year. We can't afford to pay them both unless at least one of them agrees to take a hometown discount."

Take a team like the Red Sox. They would have liked to have Johnny Damon on their roster for four more years, but not at the price he demanded. Three years was the limit they were willing to go at his price. They figured he would be a fourth outfielder by the time he entered the final year of his deal, and they weren't going to pay him superstar money. The Yankees, on the other hand, felt a couple bucks here or there, whether or not Damon would ride the pine, would be a good investment. The Yankees have the resources to retain free agents far beyond any other team in baseball, and they have the ability to outbid any other team for any free agent they may be interested in.

At that point, Dante could have gone two ways—an obscenity-laced tirade or silence indicating that he was considering all that was laid in front of him. Actually, the third option is the way he went—he got so worked up, his hair caught fire.

In the end, Dante took a step away from the ledge, which is a great start.

That's what a session with me is like. The goal is taking clients from extreme viewpoints, whether from the same planet or different solar systems entirely, and moving them away from rambling, illogical points made balancing tenuously on the Cliffs of Craziness.

For Dante, it was not a criticism, just a correction. Once on common ground, he was able to see that Martians and Uranians aren't that different. All it takes is a little understanding, some patience, and some time to get things off your chest. You might even indulge in some laughter along the way.

Like the Yankees fan who was in a room with a tiger...

Summary

"I am he as you are he as you are me and we are all together." Though neither Martians nor Uranians are a walrus or any marine-type animal, they are very similar to each other and able to relate like no other fan bases in baseball can.

The best way to soften the Martian-Uranian relationship is to meet on common ground. Writing a letter highlighting your feelings—but ultimately focusing on what it is you respect about the other—is a great idea. Plus, every minute you spend using a pen to write with is one you spend not using it as a weapon.

Think About It

Martians
Put yourself in a Uranian's shoes. Remember that episode of *Seinfeld* that featured Paul O'Neill? How many home runs did Kramer promise a little boy O'Neill would hit?

Uranians
Put yourself in a Martian's shoes. Remember that early episode of *Cheers* that featured Luis Tiant? What product was El Tiante endorsing? Can you remember the slogan and say it 10 times fast?

10

Turning Hate into "Not Quite So Much Hate"

Passion is a powerful emotion and can be either positive or negative. Hate is a very passionate emotion, as is love. I once had the opportunity to meet a wise Native American chief. I'll never forget what he told me: "It is when the hunger of the wolves in the canyon meets the fire of the mountain lion that the earth shakes under the strain of…" Actually, I have no idea what he said and what it was pertaining to. But I remember that it was very profound.

Anyway, it is with the same intensity of emotion that we achieve either love or hate.

As it takes more muscles to frown than to smile, so too does it take more to hate than to love. If you're going to be so passionate, why not lean to the right a little? It's easy and doesn't take as much energy. It even takes fewer muscles to shrug it off, suck it up, chug it down, pack it in, put it behind, check it out, see it through, think it over, and try it on than it does to hate. So why add this stress to your life?

Or you could try not being quite so passionate.

If you're worried that diminishing your passion is going to turn you into an Angels fan, allow me to put you at ease. I am not asking you to lose your passion for the game. Just back off the passion you show toward your rival planet. As another Native American chief once said,

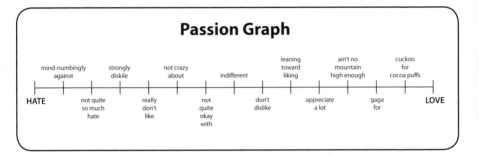

"Don't hate the player; hate the game." He may have been a vice-chief, or chief in training, now that I think about it.

Make an effort to be more accepting. Mars and Uranus orbit so closely to each other (in baseball terms, not in actual astrological calculations), it doesn't take much of a gravitational pull for them to collide. They don't need your help, so back off a little. Let each planet maintain its unimpeded rotation.

Sinner Sinner, Chicken Dinner

Not only is hate a negative emotion, but it is also one of the seven deadly sins.

It's not? Well, it should be. Let's see, Lust, Gluttony, Greed, Wrath…a-ha! Wrath! That's like hate, right? Mars and Uranus *wrath* one another. Close enough, I'm going with it.

Looking at the full list, it seems there's a lot of sin going on between the two sides.

Lust—Martians really want what Uranians have—27 championships.

Gluttony—The Yankees want more of what they've got, like a bunch o' sloppy pigs.

Greed—They both want the best players so the other can't have them.

Wrath—Martians hate the torment Uranians have put them through over the years, and Uranians hate that Martians make what should be an otherwise enjoyable existence as sloppy pigs almost unbearable.

Envy—Martians want to be able to brag like Uranians do.

Pride—Uranians constantly talk about how great the Yankees are. Martians consider the Red Sox a historic franchise, too.

Sloth—Have you met some of these fans?! The only time they've ever run is at 12:55 if the buffet is closing at 1:00. I mean, some of them have actually considered getting a catheter bag so they don't have to leave their chairs during the games. That's sloth, my friends.

Our entire existence is based on these sins. Just look at our attire, for cryin' out loud. That especially applies to the slogans and phrases we put on our T-shirts. The insulting T-shirt is a great way to see what fans are thinking by simply looking at their chests. Americans are the first culture since the ancient Romans to use garments as more than just practical skin drapes, but also for declarative statements and beliefs, usually for humorous effect.

As with everything else, shirts on Mars and Uranus are similar, yet if you look closely, you'll see slightly varying ways we project our feelings. And when hate comes out through clothing, you know there are problems.

What's in a Shirt?

In an age of abbreviated texts and tweets, of LOLs and BRBs, and of WTBTBT (went to bathroom to brush teeth), the T-shirt billboard is one of the last bastions of full-length messages. In just a few words, symbols, or phrases, an entire picture is painted. They say a picture speaks a thousand words, but each of these T-shirts paints about a dozen pictures, some which you have to be at least 18 to see.

Take a look at some of these classy Martian declarations:

> Yankee Hater
> I hate Yankees fans
> I root for two teams: the Red Sox and whoever plays the Yankees
> A*Roid
> A-Rod is an A-hole
> A-Rod, Mr. April/Miss October
> Jeter drinks wine coolers
> No Hair, No Beard, No Soul
> Yankees choked
> Yankees suck
> Take your 27 rings and shove them up your ass
> Steinbrenner Ruined Baseball

It's not exactly humor worthy of the Algonquin round table. You can see they break down into four categories—player disrespect (which goes against the cardinal rule of "Don't hate the player; hate the game"); blaming Steinbrenner for ruining the entire sport, even though he technically stayed within all rules agreed to by the owners and players' union; team disrespect; and fan disrespect.

And the shirts you'll see on Uranus are no more erudite:

> There never was a curse… they just sucked for 85 years
> We all know you're a bandwagon fan
> Big Sloppi
> Douche K

Papelbum

27 to 7

Red Sox fans: turning 86 years of frustration into 3+ years of douchebaggery

Choke: the official soft drink of the Boston Red Sox

Fenway Park: Rat infested since 1912

I root for two teams: the Yankees and whoever plays the Red Sox

I hate Boston

Boston sucks

Red Sox suck

Red Sux Nation

Fenway sucks

Celtics suck

Patriots suck

Bruins suck

Buck Foston

These, too, are not very subtle. However, they are not very well researched. For instance, a cursory check on the Red Sox home page would tell you that rats did not move into Fenway until the mid-1940s. And really, Papelbum isn't that bad. It's actually better than what some Martians call him. They say "Papelbaum," as if he's a Jewish dentist.

It's easy to see where Uranians stand in regards to their feelings of Martians and those from Mars. Though I must say I was a little curious about the "Buck Foston" shirt, so I looked him up on baseball-reference.com. Turns out, he was a weak-hitting shortstop that played two years with the Red Sox in 1953 and 1954. I'm not sure why they cared enough to make a shirt memorializing him.

Do These Come in Extra-Tasteless?

It's interesting to see the variance between the two creative mind-sets here. Martians really don't have a problem with the city of New York, any of their monuments, the landscape, the traffic, or the smell in the subway. And despite being the originators of the "suck" chants, Martians are quite sporadic about using it on cotton.

Uranians, on the other hand, take to their garment graffiti more than any other fan base. New York hates the entire city of Boston (despite the fact that many of them live there now, which might be either a geographic or vocational error they should look into) and everything in it. They hate all the teams, the players, the park, the duck boats (What kind of fascist pigs hate the duck boats, for goodness' sake?), the schools, the foliage, the public transit, and so on.

I remember a Uranian client of mine who arrived at my office, outraged after the weekend he brought his child to Fenway Park. It seems he didn't like the usage of the word *sucks*.

"They were chanting 'Yankees suck!' versus Tampa Bay before the opening pitch," he said. "I bring my five-year-old son to your venerable old park and he hears this for the first time and asks me, 'Daddy, why are they saying that bad word?' What am I supposed to say?"

He showed me a picture of him and his son with Red Sox fans seemingly yelling something toward the field in the background.

"I notice you're wearing a 'Fenway Sucks' shirt, Francis," I pointed out as he grabbed the picture away from me.

Ask the Doctor

Q: When I'm in a group of Uranians and Martians, and Mets and Phillies fans join in, what should we do?

A: Sit back and enjoy. Reminisce over how that used to be you. It's actually a good bonding experience to see how foolish they behave toward each other.

I should again reiterate that though they possess distinct personalities, Martians and Uranians sometimes swap characteristics, for example, when Yankees fans mimic shirts popularized in Boston and take a whinier stance than usual. "Everything sucks" is the point they're making, which is in direct opposition to what we've come to expect from Uranians. They usually try to portray themselves as indifferent toward Martians, but daily observation begins to show otherwise. It certainly defies the belief that they don't think about Boston as much as Boston thinks about them.

Turning the Dial Down

First, step away from the shirt press. Then just dial down the preshrunk hate rhetoric. Before you go into mass production, just soften the wording a little. Turn the hate into "not quite so much hate."

It's interesting to note that the term "Yankee Hater" was so widely used in 2004 that it was named one of the Most Politically Incorrect Phrases by the word usage group Global Language Monitor. (There's a group for that?) They suggested replacing it with the more touchy-feely term "Red Sox lover."

I've come up with some other friendlier phrases to replace the ones currently gracing torsos everywhere.

Old version	New version
I Hate Boston	I Do Not Loathe Boston
Yankees Suck	Yankees Inhale Rapidly
I root for two teams: New York and whoever is playing the Red Sox	I root for two teams: the Mets and the Yankees
I don't brake for Yankees fans	I would consider braking for Yankees fans

I'm not asking you to change your entire outlook. You do not need to make your home at the other end of the spectrum, just drive by it once in a while. Drop in for a visit. Just give it a chance to see what it's like.

Speaking of which, I had the chance to follow my own advice by visiting Yankee Stadium in 2009. I'd wanted to go for years, but was waiting for them to tear it down and put up a new one. This new one was much cleaner than the old one sitting across the street.

First and foremost, I was told to bring my checkbook as it could get quite pricey inside the Yankees' new digs. I found it curious that a ballpark would take checks, so I just brought cash. Even before I made it into the yard, I was forced to pay. Security is so tight that they don't allow bags of *any* kind (unless you're a woman, in which case you can bring a trunk full of ammunition apparently). I had a shoulder bag (okay, fine, a *man purse*, what of it?) and was told that I could not bring it inside, but I could check it across the street.

"But my bag is literally empty," I said as I opened it for them.

"Sorry, sir, it's stadium policy," the security guy said. Our conversation was going on while women were routinely being let in carrying bags so big I could've hopped inside them. ("Are you smuggling a man into the game, ma'am?" "Yes, I am." "Fine, go right ahead.") So they're not against objects you can throw, just against men carrying those objects. Well, when in New York, do as the New Yorkers do.

So I mugged a college kid in an alley. Ha ha! I kid.

The security officer pointed me to the money burn—er, bag check station, which was across the street located in "Stan's Bar." The sign outside said, "Stan the Man! Bag Check $7!" As if seven dollars for an empty bag wasn't enough, there was a *tip jar* on the counter. I guess the response they're looking for is "Thank you for taking my money. You've done such a wonderful job of it, I want you to have more."

I returned to security and showed them I no longer had my bag. They then asked me to show them what was underneath my hat. I guess that made sense, because if I were to possess a sharp object like a knife, I would definitely keep the blade pressed against my skull.

By that point it was the beginning of the second inning and I'd finally made it inside the stadium. (Unlike in Southern California where fans arrive at the games late because they think the game starts in the third inning, I now give Uranians the benefit of the doubt. They are all, most likely, stuck at security.)

Already seven dollars in the hole, I stepped up to a concession stand. They weren't kidding about the prices! I was actually handed a loan application while waiting in line for a cheesesteak. Sadly, mine was rejected and I had to settle for a hot dog. Beer, on the other hand, was relatively inexpensive. Unfortunately, cup prices were through the roof. I asked if I might just suck on the spigot, but was turned down.

I wanted to walk around and check out this new baseball palace I'd heard so much about. I was told that I had to see Monument Park, so I followed the signs but couldn't find it. I located one of those hospitality people with the "How may I help you?" paddles. He was beating a Seattle fan over the head with it.

"Monument Park is right down there," he said, pointing to a spot behind center field. "But it's closed." Fitting. I was also disappointed that I didn't get to see the "Big Papi Excavated Cursed Shirt Exhibit" at the park.

But this is not to imply that being at the park was not without its advantages. I still enjoyed myself, surprisingly, among the Yankees fans. Plus, I didn't have to listen to John Sterling yell, "An Ayyyyyyy-bomb from Ayyyyyyy-Rod."

My point is this—the experience wasn't that painful at all. Yes, the Yankees won, but I was quite serene. I was able to turn hate into "not quite so much hate." That's what I can encourage you to do as well.

I took some steps to ensure there would not be trouble. I wore my UConn hat so as not to tip them off that I was a Martian. UConn is pretty inoffensive, but just my luck, I ended up sitting behind a row of Syracuse University football players. I quickly hid my hat.

In the end, I realized things about Yankee Stadium that I didn't hate. The guy who held his garlic fries under my nose while offering them to the girls sitting in front of me, I could do without, but it was a fun—if bankrupting—evening that I would recommend to anyone. (Well, not the Seattle fans that got hung over the right-field railing by their ankles, but that goes without saying.)

Reverse Thinking

Allowing for the differences between the two fan bases, let's look at this from another angle. Would it be more fun if both sides *did* get along? Ask yourself if you would like it if Yankees fans and Red Sox fans sat together, arm in arm, watching the games in perfect harmony. Would you feel better? No. You'd be bored.

How would those conversations go?

"That was a smashing contest last night, ol' bean, between our two rooting interests, was it not?"

"Oh, I say, 'twas. I was exhilarated from the first pitch."

"And what a pitch it was. Your hurler had my slugger in dire straits, I do believe."

"Ah, it was quite the contrary, good sir. My pitcher never had a chance against your hitter."

"I beg to differ."

"You may beg all you want, but it won't help."

And then they'd laugh in a stuffy, nasal guffaw that's like nails on a chalkboard.

That isn't the way anyone would choose to go, so there *must* be a divide. There must be a yin to the yang, a bass to the treble, a Hydrox to the Oreo, and so on.

Short of loving each other—and short of shooting each other—how about just an appreciation that the other side exists and provides us with someone to berate and chastise?

Imagine how few reply posts message boards would have if everyone just agreed with one another. That would get old pretty fast. There's only so many times you can write, "I couldn't agree with you more, YanksRKing27." We need the other for, at the very least, amusement. Every great sitcom has the wise-cracking sidekick. So do we.

To use the investment metaphor again, just think of how much goodwill you'll have built up when your team falters if you simply go to the Trash Talking Bank and don't make any withdrawals. You just fill out a deposit slip for "internal smugness" and keep it in your account.

Should Uranians ever choose to waste all their savings declaring how many saves Mariano has each time Papelbon blows one, Martians will have plenty of ammo in reserve for the next time the tables are turned. Likewise, every time a Red Sox fan points out how badly the Yankees' newest free-agent pitcher is doing, the Uranians are certainly going to have retorts gaining interest in the bank.

Try Putting That on a Business Card

I am an interfanatical relationship counselor because Martians and Uranians are in a relationship, as much as they may hate to admit it. It's like a marriage, only more binding, because as hard as you may try, once you're part of one of these two "families," it's damn near impossible to distance yourself from the other.

That's why Curt Schilling sat at the podium during his introductory press conference with the Red Sox and said, "I guess I hate the Yankees now."

Yep, it's in the marriage bylaws. But I counsel not to eliminate the hate (I'm not a miracle worker), just to diminish it a little. For this, I defer to a colleague of mine, marriage counselor and author Marshall Bott. You may have read his book, *Marriage: How the Chimpanzees Have It Right*. He is world-renowned for his work on marriage counseling and has come up with the definitive work on helping marriages succeed. I take his word for it because he's been married six times, so he must know what he's talking about.

One of the things he talks about is focusing on how we influence each other. It's something you should take stock of.

Look at a Yankees fan. (Don't get too close. You don't know where he's been.) And Yankees fans, you do the same to Red Sox fans. Think about how we influence each other. Jot down some ideas—whatever pops into your head and isn't against federal law.

I'll give you one to start: we push each other to be the best. That's a given. Whether it's the teams' maniacal pursuit of Jose Contreras or the fans who came up with "A-Rod: Mr. April, Miss October," if it wasn't for Uranians, would we have even bothered?

Neither side wants to lose. We've put our energies, our desires, and our money into these Thoroughbreds and we don't want to be disappointed. If it only meant being put out to stud, that would be okay, but the repercussions of not winning are more grave to the fans who are vested, as we are, than it is for the highly paid horses.

To us, there are two teams, one prize, and it's take no prisoners. (Though there are actually 30 teams, we only care about two.)

The Five Most Important Things to Know

If you have reached this point, I can only assume you are still interested in turning hate into "not quite so much hate." There are five very simple steps to learn in order to reach your goal. They may seem to sacrifice any upper hand you may wish to keep with your rival, but I assure you, they are kid-tested and mother-approved.

Turn Toward Each Other Instead of Away

When the Red Sox won in 2004, my best friend called me. I answered the phone, which was soaked in champagne. There was a long pause, but at the end of that pause, he had issued his congratulations. I said, "Thank you. What's that I hear in the background?"

"Oh, just traffic," he said. "I'm walking along the highway trying to get hit."

I know it took a lot of guts for him to call. He certainly could've turned away from me, pretended it never happened, then after a few weeks or months had passed have brought it up as a tangent to his discussion about how great the New York Giants were.

It took guts, but he actually walked into the abuse storm he must've suspected was coming, only to realize the winds had blown the storm out to sea and there was none of the abuse that he'd expected. (A reveler grabbed my phone and tossed it into the street before I could lay the storm on him.)

Walking away only prolongs the inevitable anyway. Rip that Band-Aid off and you'll find it's never as bad as you think. (Even if a Uranian is coming at you with a car. If you head *toward* the car, you'll have more reaction time to use evasive maneuvers.)

Accountability

Taking responsibility for something stupid that you've said is generally perceived as one of the most difficult things a fan can do. The theory is that you wouldn't say something stupid if you thought it was stupid, but you didn't think it was stupid and that's why you said it.

Let's return to the Uranian that complained about Martians who are bad fans because they cannot name five players on the current roster.

Well, that may be so, but the counterpoint would be that Uranians are also bad fans because they HIT PEOPLE WITH THEIR CARS.

And I hope that doesn't come across as a "gotcha" moment. I'm not "part o' the liberal gotcha media" as Sarah Palin once said. I use it strictly to make a point. If you're going to throw stones, don't live in a glass house.

You can talk about yourself personally as a fan and maybe speak for a few others, but if you're representing the fandom and making sweeping generalizations then anything anyone else has done shows badly upon their representative—you.

Testimonial

Thanksgiving had become unbearable. If the Red Sox won, we yelled at each other. If the Yankees lost, we yelled at each other. And then we'd have a food fight. We went to the doctor and now I am best friends with my grandma. Thank you, Dr. Wasif.

—Timmy McDuggan, age 9

It's not that hard to take a little responsibility when you're wrong. Again, it's never as bad as it seems. I admit the time I hired furniture movers from in front of a liquor store was not my best decision. It did make it easier for me to move my stuff once they took all my electrical equipment and drove away with it, though.

Remember, if you're going to speak on behalf of the entire planet, then you must take the blame for any transgression that any of your fellow fans commit.

Overcome Gridlock

This harkens back to Chapter 7 and it, too, isn't easy. If you were proficient with it, you would have stopped reading by now. When there's an argument circle, you just have to get out of it. Even if there's no off-ramp in sight, take it (to paraphrase Lawrence "Yogi" Berra).

You're going to fight. It's inevitable. It could be a spirited talk meant to produce a helpful solution ("And as you can see, my health plan includes a World Series trophy for every team that participates and at very low cost to you, the fan…"), but to reiterate my instructions to you earlier, if you sense that the argument is heading in a circle, stop the bus. Say to your counterpart, "What are we doing? We're going around in a circle. Can we come to a solution without arguing?"

If the answer is "no," then at least you can agree on something. You've overcome the gridlock.

Be Tolerant of Each Other's Faults

And finally, this is the most important of all the important things to know: be tolerant of each other's faults. I refrained from putting one word into the Nation-to-Empire Dictionary in Chapter 5: *typical*. It's the last word that has two different meanings to Mars and Uranus. The word *typical* translated into Martian means "classless, ignorant, and deplorable," as in "a typical Yankees fan." In Uranian, the word translates to mean "always whining about something." Here it is in a sentence: "You are a typical Red Sox fan."

No matter which planet, in which galaxy, throughout which solar system you hail from, there is no such thing as the perfect fan. There's the craziest fan, the drunkest fan, the palest fan, and the dumbest fan, but there is no one who approaches perfection in fandom. (Though you will make strides toward becoming a better fan if you pick up my previous book, *Red Sox University*.)

Martians have faults. Uranians have faults. Who has more faults? Well, one of the faults we have is that we are constantly trying to find out. We assign a value scale to each side's faults and categorize them to come up with what seems to be a pretty legitimate system, but we still don't have an answer. We're both pretty faulty.

The point is only you can change your individual personality, And by exchanging the emotion of hate for the emotion of "not quite so much hate," you will, in fact, be doing just that. That said, to ask an entire planet to change generations' worth of emotions and belief is a little overly optimistic. To repeat my point from earlier, Red Sox fans will be Red Sox fans and Yankees fans will be Yankees fans. Just deal with it. And if counting faults makes you feel better, well, then by all means, give it a shot. (And if you get a definitive solution to that equation, I'd love to see your calculations.)

Appreciate

I'm going to sneak *appreciate* back in here. Appreciate what you have. It's not ideal, but in the end, it really isn't as bad as it could be. You could, after all, be the arch enemy of a Royals fan. What would you talk about? They're near the Negro Leagues Baseball Museum. That's kinda cool. Good barbecue places. Nice jazz. (Yawn.)

So try taking a step to the right. You'll find that even in the land of "not quite so much hate," you can still get pretty worked up. Remember, one step at a time.

Summary

At last we've come to the final frontier—shifting your feelings from one position to another, even if only slightly. In the end, that is what counseling is really for.

Shifting your feelings is all about doing the little things like wearing shirts without hurtful (though clever) insults on them, taking personal responsibility for your words instead of posting them on an anonymous Internet message board, and having enough respect for your fellow fan to say, "Hey, my brother. Let's take this outside so as not to get blood on the carpet."

Express tolerance for the other side. Leave our seven deadly sins on the doorstep and enjoy the game…until your team blows a lead in September. Then all bets are off.

Think About It

Martians

As the ultimate Christmas present, buy a Derek Jeter jersey and promise your closest Yankees-supporting friend to wear it for one entire day. Then throw it in the fireplace and burn it. Trust me, your friend does NOT want you to ever sully Jeter's image by wearing his jersey.

Uranians

As the ultimate Christmas present, buy a Dustin Pedroia jersey and promise your closest Red Sox–supporting friend to wear it for one entire day. It won't kill you (but make sure you sign that living will before you put it on).

Conclusion

So what have we learned in this paperback?

We've learned that Martians are from a very proud planet that, at one point, was the gold standard in baseball. Now, feelings of inferiority intrude on otherwise nostalgic thoughts of baseball's truest treasure—its history—and their team's former dominance.

Uranians, conversely, showed up more recently than did the Martians, and though they had some trouble at first, they eventually managed to become a totally overbearing, dominant group bent on depriving others of their riches. Power makes you feel powerful, as they say.

Overall, Martians and Uranians are not that different from one another. Both cultures fear the suicide squeeze, revere the wild card playoff system, and know that the people running the parking lots around the stadiums *say* they won't block you in, but they do. That said, there is always going to be frustration in those situations when things are going well between both worlds and then—poof!—the conversation makes a U-turn and suddenly you are dreaming of ways to flush the other guy down the toilet.

Seeking counseling should not be thought of as a weakness nor a deficiency. It's to be expected. Believe me, there are times when I've worked with a Uranian and I want to scream at the top of my lungs, "You are ruining baseball!" But I know that's not going to help. And I realize I feel this way so infrequently—mainly during the hot stove season, preseason, 19 games a year that the Yankees and Red Sox play each other, and the postseason—that it's not enough to sabotage the need for diplomacy.

We all have agendas, we all have allegiances, and we all have perceptions and opinions formulated by years of experiences, second-hand knowledge, and third-hand anecdotes. Such is the nature of Mars and Uranus.

Baby Steps

I'm not asking you to move mountains. If you could do that, I would ask you to reshape some mountains to look like Fenway Park, only with the seats facing home plate instead of the outfield.

I'm only asking you to study this guide and do the best you can to improve communication with your fellow fans. Just like when you're learning a foreign language, you're always going to have a moment when you think you are describing how embarrassed you are, but you are really announcing to the world that you are pregnant. Similarly, when you say to a Yankees fan that he is a cocky, loud-mouthed sewage weenie in an effort to insult him, you are, in fact, praising him, earning you a heartfelt "thank you."

Stay true to the tenets written here, though. If you do, I know you will weather each inning that comes your way.

Remember, you're not alone. I don't actually have a count on me, but I would estimate I've helped close to 1 million couples that have come through my door. They brought to me the same dilemmas and scenarios that you likely face and are living proof that one can go from hate to "not quite so much hate" with some professional guidance and hard work.

Be patient. We cannot assume that all these suggestions will hit the mark or that they'll be absorbed so quickly from page to heart. (Nor can we assume that Yankees fans can read.) But eventually, with practice and repetition, you *will* be able to hit it like one of those Tim Wakefield knuckleballs that refuses to knuckle.

Be brave, stand your ground, and prepare for an honest and enlightening, nonviolent discussion. (You may, however, want to tie down any loose furniture, just to be safe.)

Be judicious. Do not try to colonize the other planet. Try merely to inhabit it.

It is and will continue to be my pleasure to work toward a world where the phrase "Yankees Suck!" is replaced with the less abrasive "Yankees Are Inadequate!" or "Yankees Fans Are Overly Aggressive!" or perhaps even the more topical "Yankees Lack Bullpen Depth!" I understand the support that must be garnered before these chants can become as popular as their predecessor. But as we all know, the Big Dig wasn't dug in a day. I am under no delusions that bringing Mars and Uranus closer to one another will take years—perhaps generations—and will likely go ridiculously over budget, costing the taxpayers millions and alleviating nothing.

But imagine going to the ballpark without being consumed by hatred of your fellow sports fans, of your fellow Americans (*O Beautiful*). For when we walk alone, we are lonely (*for spacious skies*), but walk with brothers arm in arm (*for amber waves of grain*) and the glory of the Lord above (*for purple mountain majesties*) does shine on us. And so (*above the fruited plain*) we shall congregate not as regional fans, but as Americans! (*America, America*) Americans who share the same passion for the national game, the history, the emotion, the splendor (*God shed his grace on thee*). Not from a perch above the other, but at the same level, arm in arm, cheering for a spirited contest (*And crown thy good*), not caring who will win or lose (*for brotherhood*) for we are all brothers cut from the same cloth (*from sea*)—a cloth that is red, white, and blue (*to shining*) and reads "Play ball!" (*sea!*)

(Please hold your cacophonous applause for one more paragraph.)

Thank you for taking the time to read this book in order to understand your interplanetary rival. Understanding and implementing the tips I've presented to you will allow for more enjoyable interactions at the ballpark and beyond. And if it doesn't give you a respite from stressful, redundant conversations, just remember that each copy of *Red Sox Fans Are from Mars, Yankees Fans Are from Uranus* also makes a great projectile. Please buy four or five for rapid fire "conversations."

Yours sincerely,

Andy Wasif, B.S., Ph.D., O.B.P., E.R.A.

About the Author

A lifelong Red Sox fan who has collected a few Yankees fans as friends over the years (he has them mounted in his game room), Andy Wasif first focused on sports journalism before turning his attention to stand-up comedy. Fully recovered from that profession, the Syracuse University graduate has spent the last few years enjoying the teams' renewed rivalry as he studies the two fan bases and their relationship with each other. This is the third in his series of humorous Red Sox books, following *How to Talk to a Yankee Fan* and *Red Sox University*. His work is also featured in the book *The Red Sox and Philosophy*.

Andy is currently working on a memoir, along with other scripts for television and film. Visit thewasif.com for his past works and new projects, and read his blog on all things sports at sportsfanlive.com. For those tweeters out there, please follow him on Twitter @thewasif.